4 NEW MURDER CHARGES

The Standard, May 12, 1983 – 'a fresh twist in the most astonishing case of mass murder since the Moors Murders.'

In the unlikely setting of the staid London suburbs of Cricklewood and Muswell Hill, police began in February 1983 to unearth a tangled mass of human bones. Some dated back to 1979, many were unidentifiable, most belonged to transients of no fixed address and doubtful identity, all were victims of brutal killings on a systematic scale. And so began a full-scale investigation into a horrifying outrage.

THE NILSEN FI̶̶̶ the first full account of a bizarre series of crim̶̶̶̶̶̶̶̶̶̶̶ by two *Daily Mirror* journalists. Br̶̶̶̶̶̶̶̶̶̶̶̶̶ling – a tortured

le̶̶̶̶̶̶̶

Nilsen ̶̶̶ up for sale

● The attic where Dennis Nilsen murdered 15 young men is for sale, but its grisly past is being kept secret, reports the News of the World.

The £70,000 one-bedroom flat in Cranley Gardens, north London, was bought without its present owners knowing its history. A local estate agent said: "We're not telling people about Nilsen. It's nearly 10 years since all that went on."

S. TIMES

by the same authors

Brian McConnell:
ASSASSINATIONS
THE EVIL FIRM:
The Rise and Fall of the Brothers Kray
FOUND NAKED AND DEAD

Douglas Bence:
ROY JENKINS: A Question of Principle
(with Clive Branson)

BRIAN McCONNELL and
DOUGLAS BENCE

The Nilsen File

Futura
Macdonald & Co
London & Sydney

A Futura Book

Copyright © Brian McConnell and Douglas Bence
1983

First published in Great Britain in 1983
by Futura Publications, a Division of
Macdonald & Co (Publishers) Ltd
London & Sydney

All rights reserved
No part of this publication may be reproduced,
stored in a retrieval system, or transmitted, in any
form or by any means without the prior
permission in writing of the publisher, nor be
otherwise circulated in any form of binding or
cover other than that in which it is published and
without a similar condition including this
condition being imposed on the subsequent
purchaser.

ISBN 0 7088 2430 7

Typeset, printed and bound in Great Britain by
Hazell Watson & Viney Limited,
Member of the BPCC Group,
Aylesbury, Bucks

Futura Publications
A Division of
Macdonald & Co (Publishers) Ltd
Maxwell House
74 Worship Street
London EC2A 2EN
A BPCC plc Company

One

It was the kind of day when the shorn lamb hopes the Almighty is aware of the cold. Mike Cattran was. He blew on his fingers and ran them through his thinning hair to make sure he had life in both scalp and digits. For the temperature that Tuesday evening of February 8, 1983, had hovered in a chilled and showery northerly airstream just above freezing point and threatened to fall even lower.

It never had been much of a date. Historians and astrologers might have gleaned some pattern for interpretation. The Romans picked the month to be the time for purification. The English chose the date to take off the head of Mary, Queen of Scots, in 1587 and in 1750 the country actually suffered an earthquake. In 1931, elsewhere, it marked the birth day of James Dean, the actor rebel without a cause.

Now, in 1983, it was still dull. The sun, if anyone saw it, had set, the single-stalked blooms of street lamps had been turned on and it was time for the working population to go home. But not Mike. He had traversed London enough times that day, and having finished at the Ivanhoe Hotel, in the Bloomsbury of publishers and the British Museum, he headed homewards, but with little hope of a quiet evening. His girl friend, Barbara, would be waiting with a hot meal, a warm hug and comfort. Then he would wait for the next call. He was not due to be working that evening, but had agreed to stay on duty in place of a colleague who was sick.

The two-way radio under the dashboard of the red and white Ford van was not working so he parked by the first telephone he could find. The window panes were, as usual, missing and he hoped that the icy, inhospitable kiosk had not also been visited by vandals whose speciality was wrenching the handsets from the wires or at least removing the voice diaphragms. He was lucky. The dialling tone told him so.

He fingered the numbers for Control, listened, waited and pushed in a coin. Dyno-rod were on the line, the latterday Roman purifiers, the twenty-four-hours a day drain, sewer and pipe cleaners who claim, 'We are the clean leaders.'

Mike was still using his fingers as a comb and scalp masseur, shutting his eyes and thinking of home, the warm house in Clarendon Road not far from the famous Tottenham Hotspur football club, when the voice at the other end of the line snapped, 'Hold on,' and then, 'Have a look at number twenty-three Cranley Gardens over at Muswell Hill. Drain's blocked. The usual. Then check again.'

The big-boned, powerfully built caller, with the quiet manners, shrugged, said, 'Okay,' thought that was what he was paid to do, went to his van, to his A–Z street guide. He worked it out quickly, four miles from home, a traffic short cut between Hampstead and Highgate on the way to Bounds Green and Turnpike Lane, the way a good driver has to think about London's sprawl.

'Muswell Hill,' he thought. 'That's a clean drain area.' Indeed, a sort of super suburbia set on a hill almost three hundred feet above sea level looking four or five miles southwards to the great metropolis of London, to 'the Smoke'. Long before his time Muswell Hill was the spa to which the citizens of a much smaller London fled. From their hovels and dirty alleys they went to Moses' Well, whence the suburb took its name. The waters there offered relief from the King's Disease, scrofula, when the only known cure, the sovereign's personal touch, was not available or did not work.

The Hill was also a welcome milestone for the traveller who came, wary of footpads, down the Great North Road; he then knew the safety of the city was almost reached.

An 1835 local directory told the well-to-do city merchants that they should escape from the bustling city to Muswell Hill, a place for 'persons of respectability, together with dependent gardeners, laundresses and the like.' They came, first one or two, then dozens, until the end of the nineteenth century when the district was pleading to be included in the Greater London conurbation.

The pioneers complained that the houses were being built too close together, but the properties were solid ten and twelve roomed affairs where parents could have privacy, children the freedom of the nursery and the retainers a box room in which to sleep. 'I live on Muswell Hill' became the proud boast of superior commuters who felt protected from the evils of the lonely countryside and the dark of the murky London back streets.

They were apparently untouched by the noisy and often scandalous world around them. The outcry of the wrongfully convicted Dreyfus had shocked the literary and thinking world. The Turks were massacring the Armenians for the first time, Gladstone was resigning the Premiership for the last, and the Manchester Ship Canal had just been opened. It was 1894 and the foundations of Cranley Gardens were laid for a new style of suburban resident, who was willing to live in urban country rather than rural city and who was not too reliant upon the railroad.

Many Muswellians had their own carriages and regarded the railway as a courtesy for the people who used Alexandra Palace for the exhibitions, concerts and open-air recreations that took place on the south and eastern slopes of the Hill. It was not really for residents, who to be worthy of the collective title should have their own horses and conveyances.

They still had cars, Mike noticed, as he negotiated the turn into Cranley Gardens and eye-searched the gates for number twenty-three. The houses were now old, but still solid and semi-detached; some had long since ceased to be single family homes. Impoverished occupants had sold them and buyers who wanted the properties for investment had turned them, with breeze block and lath and plaster, into bed-sitting rooms, good for investment income but bad for the local image.

Bed-sitterland, usually associated with the more cosmopolitan districts such as Earls Court, the wrong part of Kensington, and other points of faded gentility, had made only occasional encroachments on to Muswell Hill and twenty-three Cranley Gardens was one of them. By comparison with the neighbouring properties it was ill-kempt. The hedge, if it could be described as such, was sparse and ragged. The path needed weeding and the mass of litter, broken refrigerators, old ovens and unusable kitchen utensils, like the frying pan without a handle, looked very out of place in the rear garden, which was also very short of flowers.

The two girls who answered the door, one auburn and forthcoming the other somewhat retiring, were not at all happy. The house, they explained, was divided into six tenancies. Apart from the girls, who had separate rooms, there was a man at the rear of the house, a fellow on the first floor, an empty apartment and another chap at the top. None of the occupants had been able to flush their lavatories, and there were three of them, since the previous weekend and the girls turned up their noses at the memory.

It was really man's talk so they summoned Jim Alcock, boyfriend of the auburn-topped lady, Fiona Bridges. He said a plumber had come on Saturday, but the caller could not complete the task satisfactorily. He had inserted cleaning machine pipes down the lavatories to clear any obstruction and had tried to drain the stack pipe at the inspection point. Unsuccessfully. Jim was entitled to be angry and to show it he waved at a door behind him and demanded to know, 'Why won't the loo flush? I just keep pulling the chain and it all comes back.' One of the girls, Fiona, nodded towards the other small room and said, 'Both of them are the same way.'

'Which inspection cap did he take off at the weekend?' Mike asked, craning his head out of the nearest toilet window, looking to see how a waste pipe from a top floor lavatory joined the runaways from the other two toilets.

'I'll show you,' Jim replied and led him downstairs, out of the house, through the rickety white gate at the side of the property to the stack pipe, which Mike banged with his screwdriver. The dull thud confirmed that the blockage was beyond the inspection point. There was only one thing to do.

He took out his torch, found the manhole cover, prised it open and recoiled from the terrible stench. He knew that his job was fundamental enough, but at this moment it reached a new bizarre low. 'It wasn't so much the smell itself that hit me,' he recalled later. 'After all, sewers seldom smell sweet. It was my instinct. That and what I saw with my torch. It was a white mass, blotched with red. It wasn't human waste.

It wasn't anything like I'd seen before. It was something from one of those television shows that carry a warning that it is unsuitable for children. What I saw wasn't fit for adults.'

Sight and smell were no help in solving the problem from a distance. Mike, holding the metal clip of the torch in his teeth, went down the twelve feet of metal rungs to the floor of the six feet by four chamber. There the waste should run down the closet pipe, through the gully cut in the floor of the cavity, then negotiate the tap into the main sewer beneath the road. The geography of such subterranean mysteries is all the same to drain men.

It was compulsive to investigate, repulsive to behold, so much so that Mike had forgotten to erect a portable fence around the manhole aperture to stop anyone tumbling in on top of him, and had forgotten all about the breathing apparatus that should be available in emergencies. The laws about health and safety at work had to wait. Soon he was recoiling from the redolent vapour.

Jim above said, 'Let's have a look. Let me see,' but he stayed firmly on top. The stench was such that Mike had to come up for air and join him, and then return with the plunger. The more he cleared of the obstruction the more followed. He thought it was raw meat, but what kind? Desperately he groped around, guided by his torch light, only to find a white conglomeration. Should it not all be red? He was eager for a component that he could recognize.

For a moment as he stood there in his overalls, Wellington boots and rubber gloves his mind went back to the summer times when he wore only swimming trunks, all that was necessary for a life guard on the Cornish sands. He had saved lives then, never lost a swimmer in trouble. But he had seen more than one body washed ashore, swollen, bruised and decomposed. Was that it? Was that the secret coming from the waste pipe?

'I thought "It's obviously not a dog. There is no fur. It's not a chicken. There is flesh, fat, gristle, slivers of skin with flesh attached. And it looks bruised." ' But he could not be sure.

Mike would have preferred to have believed that someone in the shadowy house towering above him had a freezer, had gone on holiday, switched it off by mistake. They had returned to find all their bulk-bought prime cuts of best beef, lamb, pork had gone off, bad, rancid, and covered in mildew. Foolishly they had cut it up, probably ashamed of the waste, when so many people of the Third World are starving, so ashamed that they had put it down the lavatory and flushed and kept filling the pan and flushing.

Now it moved and Mike, the below-street-level philosopher who lived on the basis that passions like fear should be subdued felt very ill. 'My bottle went,' he said.

The plumber reached the top of the ladder, reeled against the wall of the house. 'It had hair on it,' he said. 'Hair,' and kept repeating the word like a worshipper under hypnosis, over and over again. Hair.

Jim tried to be helpful. 'The guy upstairs has a dog.'

'A dog?'

Had someone killed a dog and put it down the lavatory?

Mike had to be sure. With his lungs filled with clean cold air he followed Jim back into the house, up the stairs to the top floor where the dog lived, and banged once, twice, thrice. Although there was no answer they could see a faint shadow moving behind the glass door panel. The two callers looked at each other and shrugged and were about to descend the stairs when, from behind the door came a voice, not too loud, or angry, firm but slightly querulous, the voice of a man peeved at having been disturbed.

'Who is it?'

'Oh, it's Jim from downstairs.'

The door opened slightly, a dark-eyed man, tall, clean-shaven with dark hair, peered out through metal-rimmed spectacles. He had not been sleeping. He was too alert. The face looked from Jim to Mike and back again, his rather prominent, pretty nose with the girlish ski-jump, twitching, inquiring. The eyes registered caution, the nose a question. He stood in the frame of the half-opened door reluctant to emerge, yet just as loath to retire without further information.

Mike broke the quiet. 'I'm from Dyno-rod. I understand you've got a dog.'

'Yes.' That was the only answer that seemed necessary, for the animal, a black and white mongrel, was at his feet. He could not be down the drain.

'Do you by any chance feed it fresh meat?'

'Why's that?' the man questioned the question, but went on, 'I know the drain's blocked, I wrote to the agents and complained about it.'

'Well, we seem to have found a lot of meat down the drain. That's what blocking it.'

'Not from me. I don't feed Bleep fresh meat.' He offered no more information.

As Mike and Jim turned to go downstairs the man in the door suddenly showed more interest and abandoned his unwillingness to leave his flat. He slipped on his shoes and followed the callers. The other tenants had gathered on the first-floor landing, chatting, glad that the managing agents had said it was all right to spend the money on cleaning the drains, delighted that without further ado they had called in the plumber. The saviour. And hopeful that he had a solution.

12

Mike ignored them and walked slowly to the pay 'phone. They watched and listened as he called the supervisor at home.

'Gary? Mike. Sorry to bother you, but you're not going to believe this. I'm at Cranley Gardens and I've found a body, or what remains of a body, down a drain, down the manhole. Shall I call the police?'

As he spoke he turned to those on the landing beside him, searching for any reaction.

'Wait a minute,' said Gary at the other end of the line. 'Don't make a fool of yourself, Mike. Have you thought of all the possibilities of what it might be?'

'Yes,' said Mike emphatically.

'Are there any Pakistanis living there?' As if Pakistanis had a habit of putting bodies down drains.

'No, Gary, there aren't.' Mike was showing signs of slight irritation.

'Is it tied in with any other houses?'

'No, Gary. I know what I've found.'

'You're sure.'

'Yes.'

'It'll take me at least an hour to get there.'

'Shall I call the police meanwhile?'

'Is it going anywhere? Is it going to disappear?'

'No.'

'Don't call the police now. Everything looks different in daylight. Wait till morning. I'll come round with you first thing.'

Reluctant, resigned, feeling guilty that he had for once been talked out of a commonsense argument, Mike turned to the anxious group and explained, 'Don't worry about it. I'll be back first thing in the morning.'

The tenants were unconvinced. They watched as he turned his back, went outside and, changing direction, went to the manhole cover once more. Mike paused,

13

conscious of a second figure at his right shoulder. It was the man from the top flat, armed with a torch.

'So you've got a torch as well, have you?'

The man did not answer.

'So you've got a torch as well, have you?' Mike repeated the question. Ignored a second time Mike shrugged his shoulders and went down, pausing to listen to the series of questions the top flat dweller fired at Jim from the first floor. 'How will they clear it? How will they get rid of it? How are they going to get it all out?' The questions came in an unblocked stream. 'I suppose they'll get the council to suck it out, put it in plastic bags, or maybe pump it out.'

Jim answered him. 'No, I don't think so. They'll just push it all into the sewer.'

Mike remained silent. He took a last look round the chamber to reassure himself that he had not been mistaken, shuddered and came up for what he hoped would be the last time, devouring again the sharp chill air as he replaced the manhole cover. Then he clambered into his van and began the four mile drive home. All the way, at every gear change, at every touch of the brake pedal he wanted to turn the vehicle round and return to Cranley Gardens. The secret of the blocked drain must still be in the house, in one of the six apartments, locked in the minds and hearts of one or more of the occupants.

Could this be real? It was, after all, Muswell Hill, not the sort of place where anything sinister occurs. The local antiquarians would admit that a girl who found herself pregnant without a husband committed suicide and was buried at the crossroads with a stake through her heart as a warning to other wantons. Two men had been hanged for burgling the home of a wealthy engineer and murdering him by beating him to death. That was all long, long ago, in another century.

Nothing as sensational had occurred in the vicinity since. Until now, 1983.

Despite the heat in the van Mike shivered at the evening's events. He had performed a public duty and then wondered if he had behaved correctly in putting off the matter until the morning. He kept telling himself, 'If I don't go back I'll never know the truth.'

At home he tried to explain to Barbara, his understanding girl friend, that there was something sinister behind the blocked drain at Cranley Gardens. She listened sympathetically, said it would be all explained in the morning, and would he, please, come to the table to eat his supper. He did not eat any supper, had three large whiskies and was called out on another job.

Next morning, Wednesday, back at Cranley Gardens, watched by Gary, Mike lifted the manhole cover and paused. With a sudden heave he pulled it away to reveal a clean, flushed drainage system of which any householder, any health inspector, any man from Dyno-rod should be proud. There was nothing there. Absolutely nothing. And Mike, far from being relieved, was very angry and felt not a little silly.

'I told you we should have dealt with it last night. Who's made a fool of himself now?' he shouted at his supervisor. He did not wait for an answer, but half ran to the front door and began punching the bell buttons. To each of those who answered, he demanded, 'Did you call any other firm after I left here last night?'

'No. Why?' one tenant answered.

'Because what was down there last night has gone.'

'That's funny. There was someone down there last night, working.'

'What d'you mean, working?' Mike asked of the talking head.

'I don't know. I kept hearing noises as if someone was working underground.'

Mike assumed command of the tenants. 'Now don't run any water! Don't flush any toilets! Is that understood?' he ordered.

Mike was resolute, Gary from Control was quizzical. Mike dropped down the manhole and wondered whether, even now, Gary believed him. He stood, feet astride the gully, and noticed the water in the interceptor was grey, the sort of colour that comes from mixing fat with water, but the solid matter had disappeared. Who knew it was there? Only he, only Gary, only the tenants, those who had listened to his telephone conversation the previous evening had that knowledge, only the person who put it there. They were the only people who knew the secret of the drain and could have come down in the night to clean it out.

As he examined the pipe that came down from the house and the trough beneath his feet, his thoughts were interrupted by a girl's voice. He clambered up the iron ladder until his shoulders were at ground level and he could look along the gravel at the slippered feet padding towards him. They belonged to Fiona, the russet haired girl, who was pulling a winter coat over her dressing gown, not so much protection against the shivering morning, but like the cloak of fear.

Fear talks. Her words spattered the air, but were perfectly coherent. 'We heard noises in the night. That is, my boy friend and I. Jim. There was someone going up and down the stairs all night. He, my boy friend, was so worried that he went to look for whoever it was with an iron bar. And he saw the guy from upstairs on the landing in his shirt sleeves going in and out of the toilet where he was flushing again and again.'

The plumber, now out of the drain, walked slowly round the house until he could see the window of the top flat, as if expecting to see a shadow, a moving figure, a swift movement of the curtain, a pair of eyes.

16

All he saw, despite the freezing air, was a strangely open window.

'Don't worry,' he said. 'Calm down. Go and call the police. And make us a cup of tea.'

Once more Mike climbed down the cellar rungs, put his hand inside the interceptor trap and searched. He pulled out a piece of flesh, bruised and cut, then three or four pieces of bone. He held them up in his hand and measured them against his other paw. They were the top joints of human fingers. Two from the tips to the first knuckle, two from the knuckle to the second joint. He was sure of it.

Two

Detective Chief Inspector Peter Jay is a big active officer of forty-six years, measures six feet two and a half inches and at sixteen and a half stone has the shape of a heavyweight boxer. He makes no pretence of championship ability, but any man twenty years younger would be wise to calculate his chances before picking a physical quarrel.

On that Wednesday morning he looked incongruous sitting in his first floor office at Hornsey police station. He looked out of the window at the shoppers in Tottenham Lane girding themselves against the cold and was not glad to be confined to his office desk. Sifting through a mountain of papers was not only boring. It meant being imprisoned in an office waiting for a knock on the door, for the telephone to ring, for any kind of summons that would take him outside. His eyes kept wandering to the carver chair opposite him.

If he was not called out there would soon be someone to occupy it, a superior with a re-direction about prosecution not necessarily in the public interest; an inferior to be encouraged to talk, explain and be admonished; a member of the local council dissatisfied with the way his ward is being policed. He had seen them all before and would again. But he did not expect anything like the next call.

'Detective Chief Inspector,' he said, picking up the instrument the moment it began to shrill.

'Mr Jay,' said the officer from the front desk downstairs. 'Radio call for you from Inspector Slade. Wants assisting at twenty-three Cranley Gardens. Says a plumber reckons he's found some human remains down a blocked drain.'

The Chief Inspector glanced at his watch as he pulled on his three-quarter length sheepskin coat from the office corner coat stand. It was just before 10.50 a.m. He booked out an inconspicuous unidentifiable car from the garage yard and drove the mile to the address on the south-western slopes of Muswell Hill. He raised his eyebrows in greeting to Inspector Slade, the uniformed officer on duty, who indicated the key man waiting for him, Mr Cattran, the plumber.

'Are you the chief inspector they said was coming?' The plumber's voice had a tone of hostility. Mike resented authority most of the time but today it was born of frustration rather than rebellion. First he had not believed what he had found. Then Gary had not credited him with telling the truth. Now the police seemed unexcited, unmoved. Yet he had smelled the samples, seen then, felt them and picked them up.

Twelve hours before he had told the beginning of the story and his fears to his girl friend Barbara. She had said they would all be explained the following day. Already the drain had been cleared, the bones found behind the interceptor and the promised explanation was still not there. Surely the police would believe him. None of them had gone down the drain to investigate. He looked up at Jay's bulk and felt a little better. It belonged, after all, to a Chief Inspector.

'What do you make of these?' asked Mike, crouching down to the little pile of bones lying by the open drain. Jay did as Mike had done. He picked up the lifeless digits and matched them for length against his other hand.

'It looks like a knuckle joint on each,' he said. Mike

19

felt much better, but Jay, without another word, disappeared into the house. Going methodically from door to door, asking questions, he took fifteen minutes to learn all he could for the present and it was enough. He knew that a man called Nilsen lived in the top flat, knew that the blockage in the drains could be traced directly and only to his lavatory, and that he had been seen in his shirt sleeves during the night going in and out of the first floor toilets, flushing, then going to the drain outside, poking about among the detritus, then returning to flush the toilets again. It must have saved him the extra journey flushing both toilets with water on the first floor instead of climbing to the top of the house to pull the chain on only one.

Cattran was left to finish the job for which he had been summoned in the first instance. 'When you have done here,' a policeman called to him, 'would you mind going down to Hornsey police station to make a statement?'

When Cattran left the house in Cranley Gardens at about 11.30 that morning he still wondered whether the case was being treated with the importance it merited. The strip of flesh and the finger joints he had collected were still lying in the bottom of a cardboard box which had once contained a supply of yoghurt. Should not someone put it in a plastic bag and label it as they did in television detective films? Perhaps the case was not unique and they had lots of calls like this and they were kept secret from the ears of reporters and the eyes of cameras.

It was no better at the police station where he was only interviewed by a detective constable. He was disappointed. Only when the chief inspector put his head round the door of the interview room did Mike feel temporarily important, that he had been of public service.

'Get down everything you can about what he found,' Jay told the constable. 'Size, shape, description. The lot. We want to know everything.'

The information went only one way. The constable told Mike nothing. His eyes focused on the bridge of his nose, unblinking, unscanning. At the end of the interview, during which Mike was asked to draw what he had found, the officer thanked him, said, 'We'll be in touch,' and showed him the door. The old doubts returned. They did believe him, didn't they.

Jay most certainly did, but he was not saying anything to anyone, except his chief. No, he did not want to see Mr Cattran again, not yet. He wanted to interview Nilsen, but he was not at home and no one knew his business or where it was conducted. As for those bones, he supposed they were human, but he needed expert confirmation.

Professor David Bowen could tell him, but the forensic pathologist was not at the local mortuary. He was at the new Charing Cross Hospital across London at Fulham Palace Road, Hammersmith, either lecturing on the doctors' contribution to murder investigations or being consulted by another police officer about another corpse. Jay sighed, put the bones which he had collected from the drain and sealed in a plastic bag on the passenger seat of his car and drove himself to Hammersmith.

'They are human,' said the professor and by two o'clock in the afternoon suggested the sex and age of the owner.

With that information the chief inspector collected two more officers, Detective Inspector Steve McCusker and Detective Constable Geoffrey Butler, drove to Cranley Gardens to wait for Nilsen. Fiona Bridges let them into the house. A barmaid at the nearby Royal Oak public house, she was more than helpful, made them tea and went over the experiences of the last few days once again.

Jay went to the top flat, peered through the frosted glass panel of the door and inspected the lock. Nilsen's dog, Bleep, started barking. Aware of what police dogs can do to sheepskin coats and the wearers the chief inspector withdrew and waited for Nilsen in Fiona's flat.

Just before 5.30 p.m. they heard the key in the front door lock. Jay was across the hall floor before the homecomer could close the door behind him.

'Mr Nilsen?'

'Yes.'

'I'm Detective Chief Inspector Jay from Hornsey C.I.D. I've come about your drains.'

Nilsen's face, though puckered from the cold outside, did not register surprise. 'Why are you interested in them?' asked Nilsen after a pause.

'You take me up to your flat and I'll tell you.'

'Well, you'd better come up,' said Nilsen, turning to the stairs, leading Jay, McCusker and Butler to the top. All three policemen waited patiently as Nilsen's trembling hands struggled with the key in the lock and announced to the once more barking Bleep that his master was home.

'Are they health inspectors?' said Nilsen, nodding towards Jay's companions.

'No, they're police officers.'

Jay did not take his eyes from Nilsen's hands as the tenant led them first into the kitchen, then right into the sitting-cum-bedroom, untidily and poorly furnished with little more than a bed, a couple of arm chairs, a table and a television set.

'Mr Nilsen,' said Jay quietly, 'the drains are blocked with human remains.'

Nilsen looked surprised. 'Oh my God, how awful.'

The chief inspector stared hard at Nilsen, pushed his nose up close to his and snapped, 'Now don't mess about, Nilsen. Where's the rest of the body?'

'They're in two plastic bags in the other room. I'll show you,' the occupier replied, and began walking to the door.

'I thought so. What's been going on here?'

'It's a long story. I'll tell you everything.'

Jay, already conscious of the smell that had been aggravating his nose since the moment he entered the flat, knew that what he would put in his report was the 'recognizable aroma' of decomposing flesh. There was no doubt that the man who had just come home for tea was telling the truth.

'No! Don't show me now,' said Jay. 'I'm going to arrest you on suspicion of murder.'

The standard legal formula followed, the official caution, known to everyone stopped for a traffic offence and to every watcher of television thrillers. Jay told Constable Butler to remain in the flat and motioned Inspector McCusker to come with him, sandwiching Nilsen between them as they went down stairs and out of the house to the police car.

Jay glanced at his watch as he climbed into the driving seat. It was not yet 5.45 p.m. less than seven hours since he had been called to the case, and here was the murderer in the back seat with McCusker on the way to the police station.

Down Cranley Gardens, right into Park Road, rolling gently down to the clock tower at Crouch End they went. McCusker was thinking hard about the improbable conversation in the upper flat. 'Where's the rest of the body?' the chief inspector had asked. Nilsen had answered, 'They're in plastic bags in the other room.' The inspector looked at the back of Nilsen's head as the prisoner gazed unconcernedly out of the window at the passing traffic. 'Are we talking about one body or two?' McCusker interrupted his thoughts.

'Neither, it's sixteen.'

Nilsen did not bother to turn round. Jay swore. His hands left the wheel momentarily. The car swerved into the oncoming lane as a fast approaching vehicle swerved away from him. In a second he regained control, looked in the driving mirror at McCusker, and with one of those warning looks policemen exchange, closed the conversation. McCusker understood, nodded and continued to watch the quiet mass murderer at his side.

Three

An emergency '999' call in the morning, a preliminary pathologist's report just after lunch, and an arrest at tea time augured well for a mass-murder investigation, but Chambers gave little sign of pleasure. Detective Chief Superintendent Geoffrey Chambers, chief of 'Y'-for-Yankee Division, C.I.D., had spent thirty of his fifty-one years in the Metropolitan Police. All that time on the beat, in the Criminal Investigation Department, in the Serious Crimes Squad, Interpol, in the Fraud Squad and even in the Internal Complaints Investigation Branch had left him with no time for surprises or assumptions.

When he walked that Thursday morning across the garage yard of Hornsey police station with Jay, he gave, as always, the impression that he was slouching. They were different shapes and sizes, but even so, where Jay looked poised for action on the balls of his feet Chambers looked vague, preoccupied with some totally different subject on his mind. 'All fag ash and confusion' as he was known affectionately by his team, a team that knew it is a front.

If a television producer was offered Geoffrey Chambers as a fictional detective character for a series he would reject the idea. Kojak, Colombo, even Sherlock Holmes are all more believable people. They suck lollipops, wear dirty raincoats and work out computer-sized problems in their minds. Chambers deals with reality without razzamataz. He conducts investigations like a poker player with a permanent royal flush in his hand and the pot in his pcoket, never showing.

Even with someone as close to him as Jay, his chief inspector, he maintains his style. Even as they entered the office for the momentous interview with the mass killer the chief said, 'What did you say this fellow's name was?'

'Nilsen, guv'nor. N-I-L-S-E-N.'

The prisoner was brought in by two constables. Chambers looked up at the five feet eleven inches, twelve stones of featureless man. His sheet from the doctor showed that he had no tattoos, no birth marks. He was not outstanding, whatever Jay had said he had done. He could lose himself in a crowd. Indeed, if the police had been equipped with his description and had to look for Nilsen in a murder hunt they might never have found him at all.

Operationally, Chambers worked by the rule book from the first to the last page and he insisted that his team did the same. At 10.30 a.m. Chambers nodded to Jay who motioned Nilsen to the carver chair on Chambers' left, their backs to the wall. Jay sat at his desk facing them, a police pad in front of him, and began. 'Mr Chambers is going to ask you questions so that we can prepare a statement. I am going to write everything down. You have plenty of time. At the end you can read it all through and sign it.'

The chief superintendent lit a cigarette, gazed vacantly at the ceiling until he had inhaled. Almost as an afterthought he offered one to Nilsen, then said suddenly, 'Your full name, please?'

Dennis Andrew Nilsen.'

'Your date of birth?'

'November the twenty-third, nineteen forty-five.'

'Where was that? Where were you born?'

26

'At Fraserburgh, in Scotland. Forty-seven Academy Road.'

That was the beginning of nine interviews lasting a total of thirty-one hours, Chambers, giving the lie to any idea that his mind was ever vague, served questions, sometimes slowly, sometimes at the rate of machine gun fire, always carefully worded and even when Nilsen hesitated always reminded him politely that at the end he would be given time to read, understand and agree or disagree before he added his signature.

As Jay's fountain pen scratched down the answers there were frequent interruptions. Occasionally a cadet would be summoned to bring tea. At other times either Chambers or Jay would leave the room to confer directly or by telephone or radio with members of the murder squad, deploying them on a new line of enquiry or asking for a report on what progress had been made. And there were meal breaks.

Nilsen was 'coughing well' in police parlance, making a full and frank confession, but Chambers knew he was not going to have all that easy a time substantiating or refuting some of Nilsen's ghastly claims. What he was saying for much of the time would test the credulity of more than the most suspicious policeman. It seemed that every amazing question had a more astonishing answer.

Earlier, when Mike Cattran, the plumber, had told his story he had come up against a similar reaction. Doubt.

As a result, he felt the need to talk, to get it off his chest. He began by telephoning one popular newspaper and asking, 'Are you interested in a story about some bodies that have been found down a drain?'

'Hang on!' said a voice. There was a long pause, then 'I don't think so.'

'Or bits of bodies?' he persisted. 'Enough to fill four buckets?'

'Hang on!' Another pause. 'No thanks.'

'All right, mate, but you're going to hear about them, I can tell you.' The papers. They were worse than the police. What was wrong with them? Was not the finding of human remains in a drain important? Is it not news?

There had to be somebody interested. He called Frances Hardy. She is petite and pretty, twenty-six years of age, and a reporter. A local reporter, true, but she is an astute listener, and a persuasive questioner, always on the alert for something more than the winner of the home-made jam contest at the local church bazaar. Mike knew her well because Frances and her boy friend often joined Barbara and him for a foursome outing, for a drink and a meal when funds and fancy suggested it.

Now Frances cupped her small face in one hand, let her long hair fall over her shoulders as she stared in fascinated horror at the telephone through which Mike related his tale. She understood. She made notes. And Mike felt much better.

The story was of no value to her local newspaper, the *Bishop's Stortford Gazette*. The hideous happening was more than thirty miles out of its circulation area in Hertfordshire, but it was too good a yarn to ignore. Like Mike she wondered, 'who will believe it?' She quickly made up her mind. She would tell Fleet Street and it would be both rewarding and instructive to see what the occupants of that avenue of adventure would make of it.

In her notebook she wrote just forty-four words which she hoped would send editors screaming for more and reporters scurrying for minutiae. She dictated, 'A chopped-up corpse was discovered in a North London manhole by a plumber on Tuesday. Mike Cattran of Tottenham was called to clear a blocked drain at Cranley Gardens, N.10. He discovered decaying lumps of flesh blocking the pipe. More details if required.' She called five popular national tabloids with the same message and literally hit Fleet Street in the breadbasket. For which editor would serve up such a story? In the bitter competition for circulation and profits there is still, strangely, a fear of upsetting the digestion of the breakfast-time newspaper reader. As a result more than one editor prayed that the story was untrue or there would be some reason for not telling the story to the public.

To the newspaper industry the 'story of the day' is very much like 'the dish of the day' in a restaurant, too often unchangeable. That Wednesday night for Thursday morning's papers the big story concerned the theft or kidnapping of Shergar, the famous thoroughbred racehorse in Ireland. Owned by a syndicate headed by the Aga Khan, its disappearance had shaken students of the turf, animal lovers and more. That kind of story in newspaper parlance could only be 'killed' or shifted from the front page by the elopement of the Pope and little else.

Even the popular Princess Diana, wife of the heir to the throne, had only very recently earned a rest from newspaper coverage because of the disappearance of that horse. Now Shergar too was threatened with demotion because someone had found some bones in a North London drain. Such is fame.

Scotland Yard did not know of the find. At least they professed ignorance, and eventually it was left to the persistence of one or two newspapers to mention the matter in a paragraph or two. Only the *Daily Mirror* –

with a story written by Douglas Bence, co-author of this volume – went so far as to tell the skeleton of the story at some length on page five with white lettering on a black strip: 'Plumber's grisly discovery starts murder inquiry', and below it, in inch-plus high characters, 'CUT UP CORPSE IS FOUND IN DRAIN.'

The story, like the weather, numbed many senses for a while and then as the new day broke, more reporters, photographers, radio interviewers and television cameramen swarmed to the scene, searching Cranley Gardens for the secrets of the great calamity. Perhaps another series of Moors murders with that overtone of child torture which challenged the belief of the nation in 1966, or even another Yorkshire Ripper, who had managed between 1975 and 1980 to murder thirteen women, mostly prostitutes, and injure several more. The usually quiet thoroughfare was, in the poet's words, maddened to crime.

As the media people huddled in the freezing atmosphere, stomping their feet, cracking their knuckles and gossiping with neighbours and curious bystanders, the police recovered considerably more human remains than Nilsen had threatened to show Jay and company the previous evening. The first find was exactly as Nilsen had described, in two plastic sacks thoughtfully supplied by the local council and carrying the slogan, 'Keep Haringey tidy.' In addition there were an assortment of containers with more pieces of bodies. Every now and then a detective would flash open a lid for an instant pretending something unspeakable was inside. The macabre jollity soon turned to sourness when officers moved from the house a coffin.

It contained recognizable pieces of a body, butchered and then boiled beyond easy identification. In addition police took away three severed heads, all of which had

30

been boiled, a sight that was to put more than one policeman off his canteen food for the rest of the day.

Inside the house everything was photographed from every conceivable angle. There were clues galore, but fingerprinting, the most basic detective discipline, was impossible. The flat windows had been left open and the place was as damp as a mediaeval prison cell. That condition held the investigation in Cranley Gardens in abeyance for twenty-four hours while heaters were brought in to dry the moisture-covered surfaces. That process left a forensic feast of latent tell-tale prints which were to confirm many of Nilsen's bizarre stories about the identity of victims who had entered his flat and what had become of them.

In the days that followed, the apartment was dissected, floor board by floor board. Even the plaster came off the wall. The entire flat was dismantled as though it were a do-it-yourself assembly kit in reverse. And the drains, now cleaned, were subjected to closer attention. Police invited a firm which specializes in looking round corners to call at Cranley Gardens. A crew, equipped with miniature television cameras, the lenses less than two inches in width, mounted on skis that can turn corners in places like waste pipes, filmed what went on round the bend. The resultant colour video tape of the search produced more clues, including human teeth and fingers.

Twenty-three Cranley Gardens was declared a no-go area. Police had little difficulty in persuading the residents to move out and sleep elsewhere. No one wanted to stay when they heard what had occurred in the top flat. Then came an alarm that shook even the visitors. Hospital records showed that one of Nilsen's last victims had been treated for hepatitis. The policemen on duty did not have to be told that the disease of the liver is highly infectious, the death rate from it high. It arises in a number of ways and is picked up very easily, especially by those with no settled home, no regular habits and no fixed diet. It attacks the liver, and can reduce the sufferer to a coma and even death. In 1983 it had become very much the vagrants' disease. One London magistrates' court had to be held in the open air when a hepatitic down-and-out appeared on a charge. In York, where police had to provide an exclusive cell for such a person, the prisoner died and the local pathologist – satisfied that there was no evidence of foul play – decided it would be dangerous even to carry out a post-mortem on some organs of the dead man.

Professor Bowen of Charing Cross Hospital was consulted and confirmed the presence of hepatitis in some of the organs he had under the microscope. A professor from St Thomas's Hospital was called to advise on the public health risk. Health authorities were anxious not to make the discovery public. Panic could well follow. Instead, anyone who had been in the house, permanently or temporarily, particularly the plumber and policemen who had handled remains, were ordered to see a doctor. All were subsequently given a clean bill of health.

By then police were ready to seal the house of death. The last to try to sleep there was Nilsen's dog. On the night Nilsen was arrested the two uniformed constables on the door had heard his pathetic whine and took him first to Hornsey police station and then to Battersea Dogs' Home, the London sanctuary for animals without a home or master.

The house became a monument to horror, windows barred, doors padlocked against the adventurous or ignorant squatters and in the months ahead it became little more than a stopping-off point for Women's Institute mystery tours, much to the chagrin of the respectable residents who remained in that Muswell Hill avenue. The property had been fumigated so it ceased to be a health hazard but it had to wait for the trial of its notorious occupant before any claim for the restoration of the upstairs flat could be entertained.

Cranley Gardens was surely enough to investigate, but as the questions and answers kept flowing in Chief Inspector Jay's office that Thursday morning a further problem arose. The number of dead. Chambers kept nagging at Nilsen and adding up on his fingers. Killer and detective finally agreed: it was fifteen, not sixteen. The chief superintendent held up a cigarette, pointed it at Nilsen and said, 'Do I understand you correctly? Now we've got the number right, are you saying you murdered three people at Cranley Gardens and another twelve persons at a previous address, before you moved to Muswell Hill?'

'Yes,' said Nilsen in a tired voice.

'Where was that address?'

'One nine five Melrose Avenue, Willesden.'

Chambers jerked his thumb towards the door and Jay lumbered out to tell the murder squad to begin investigating the newly discovered address. Chambers stubbed out his half smoked cigarette, lit another and checked to see he had enough in his packet to last the next round in the recitation of murder. The murder squad knew what to do.

Willesden, like Muswell Hill, is the essence of suburban anonymity. Both were originally in Middlesex but have long since fallen within London's massive political and administrative spread. Both developed around old watering holes. Just as Moses' Well became Muswell Hill so Willesden derived its name from Wellesdone, and both had long been dry.

The rolling Willesden acres were turned into comfortable homes with easy access roads, and if there was any real difference it was that Muswell Hill relied more on people having their own carriages while Willesden beckoned because of the arrival in the area of the Metropolitan line railway. Every carriage was to be fitted with the legend over the door handle, 'Live in Metroland', and children were to skip down their newly found suburban streets to the rhyme:

> Take a sympathetic hand to
> Willesden, Harrow, Wembley,
> Dreaming isles of Metroland.

Melrose Avenue was a product of that thinking in 1896. Prospectors were finding gold in the Klondike. Jameson's raiders had been beaten off by the Boers. But six years were to pass before the road was completed by which time the Boer War was over and the peace treaty signed. The new suburbanites moved in. They were the kind of people who had once dreamed of an acre of land and a cow apiece as a mark of respectable citizenry, but now wanted quarter of an acre and a maid.

Like the first occupants of Cranley Gardens they were those from the comfortable sector of the population, the ophthalmic surgeon, the vicar, the rabbi, the professor of violin and the teacher of pianoforte. Only in one respect did Melrose materially differ. It had a complex of hard tennis courts and the gardens were larger, allowing more planning and more cultivation.

Then the fascination which had surfaced at Muswell Hill was felt at Willesden. Residents who usually keep themselves to themselves came out shivering into the cold, eager to know the sinister story in the air. Silently they watched as the scaffolding was erected, first to support the plastic sheeting over the back garden and

34

then to provide a mounting for the arc lights that would illuminate the tiniest of finds.

Into this macabre, makeshift 'greenhouse' came a legion of policemen in green boiler suits, carrying spades, sieves and a mass of heavy-duty plastic bags. Behind them, a few days later, came a nursery of thirty police cadets, boys and girls not long out of school, who had to go down on their hands and knees to search the outback, grass blade by grass blade, until they ran out of land beyond the garden. The enthusiasm of both senior and junior diggers and searchers seemed somewhat in advance of their skills as they went to work with a will, for no one could say how much eagerness was to find clues to yet another murder and how much to exercise their muscles against the cold.

Their frenzied activity, as shown on television, brought a sharp rebuke from Mr Tim Tatton-Brown, director of the Canterbury Archaeological Trust, who wrote to *The Times* that the dig 'shows once again how incredibly crude some police "forensic" work is . . . the bones that are found are usually thrown into a bag or box and "taken to a pathologist" . . . Were the police to call in some professional archaeologists to advise them it would probably be quicker, cost less and produce more evidence.'

An academic censure perhaps, but then the police were accustomed to such brickbats. On top of all the criticisms and demands for public accountability, here was a different case, a case of mass murder which had been virtually solved, so far as the detectives were concerned, in twenty-four hours.

The good public image of the police had to be maintained and part of this task fell to Stuart Goodwin, a deputy press officer in Scotland Yard's large public relations division. His particular task was to act as liaison officer between the criminal investigators and the media at Melrose Avenue. As in most cases, the detectives would not be anxious at such an early state of the investigation for much information to be released, and the hungry hordes of the media were bound to be dissatisfied.

On Thursday afternoon while they waited for information, Goodwin was dispatched to Kilburn police station, a temporary headquarters for part of the investigation. There he was told to wait until a senior officer could brief him on what he might tell and what he might not. He went to the canteen and while sipping a cup of tea learnt a little more of the task ahead, to his consternation. From the next table came voices.

'Did you hear about the business up in Melrose Avenue?'

''Course I did. The whole nick's full of it.'

'You know who it is, don't you? That guy, Nilsen, used to be on The Job at Willesden Green. One of ours, for Christ's sake.' The Job. Police jargon for the daily work they do.

Goodwin wondered if and how he would have to reveal eventually to the public that Dennis Andrew Nilsen, of Cranley Gardens and formerly of Melrose Avenue, now answering questions at Hornsey police station about anything from one to sixteen murders or more, was once a policeman, stationed at Willesden Green. 'One of ours, for Christ's sake.'

The conversation continued.

'He hasn't been on this patch since I've been here.'

'No. This is ten years ago. Something like that. He was only a copper for a year or so, but I remember him.'

'Has he been heard of since?'

'I think he's been in the book a couple of times.

36

Poofter. Domestics. Nothing serious. No action taken. The usual.'

'Well, it's a bit serious now by all accounts.'

'Not half. We'll find out soon enough. At least one of the blokes here trained at the same time as him.'

Goodwin listened, then left, saw the uniformed commander in charge of the division, listened to the briefing and went to Melrose Avenue. The investigation there was not made easier by the fact that Nilsen had had a wider range for his operations. He had had access to the garden, while at Cranley Gardens his tenancy had restricted him to the house.

The 'big dig' at Willesden lasted thirteen days and nights. The garden and the land were turned over, the interior of the newly modernised and redecorated dwelling taken apart. It produced clues galore, fragments including human bones, a certain piece of rib, part of a hip bone, a jawbone with teeth intact, six inches of thigh bone, a cheque book, a pen, pieces of clothing, a silver medallion.

As each exhibit was taken from the house, docketed, photographed, entered into the register, the speculation about how many bodies had been identified or were likely to be accounted for grew to exaggerated proportions.

Chambers and Jay were keeping Nilsen's figure of sixteen to themselves, but they still had difficulty in believing him. His memory had its shortcomings. Besides, there was no corroborative evidence for much of his story at Melrose Avenue because there were traces, even after such an elapse of time, of three funeral pyres. They had thrown up charred remains but hardly enough to identify their former owners, barely sufficient to help a pathologist determine the cause of death.

Neighbours recalled their complaints to the local

council about the number of bonfires a tenant had started at night, causing unpleasant smoke and smells to disturb them, but nothing had been done about it and the nuisance did not stop until October 1981 when Nilsen took £1,000 from the would-be developer of the property as an incentive to move out, had one last blaze and moved to Cranley Gardens the day after.

The lack of corroboration and the fear that some of the bodies would never be positively identified prompted Scotland Yard to issue a public appeal. 'Tell us if your son is missing. Telephone us on 01-348 5201, Extensions 35 and 36,' said a Metropolitan Police poster and it was repeated *ad infinitum* by newspapers, radio and television stations.

For those who sought more information, without personal reasons, Goodwin could tell them little more. 'Police are investigating more than one murder,' was all he was permitted to state.

'How many more?'

'More than one.'

Later, after conferring with Chambers, Scotland Yard declared that 'until the search of Cranley Gardens and the digging and search of Melrose Avenue is completed we shall not know how many bodies, or if there are any more bodies.

'Although we have been given the names of at least two people who we believe are dead and whose remains may be found in one of the two houses, or in the vicinity, we have no other details about them. We do not have a list or anything like that. You must remember we are going back at least three years. It is for that reason that we are checking on missing persons going back some years, as far back as 1978 and beyond that. At the same time a careful note is being made of every person who, as a result of the publicity given in this case, is inquiring after a missing person no matter how long ago they disappeared.'

At Hornsey police station Chambers was frustrated. He had numbers but wanted names.

'How many people did you say you murdered?' he asked Nilsen again.

'Fifteen,' was the prompt reply.

The chief superintendent offered the prisoner another cigarette, took one himself and rolled a third across to Jay.

They all looked exhausted but the meticulous Chambers inhaled and said, 'All right, Mr Nilsen, let's go back to the beginning and start again.'

Four

A man arrested on suspicion of having committed a crime cannot be held in custody for more than forty-eight hours without a charge being brought against him. That's what the rule book says. Mr Chambers believes in the rule book, works by it, so he looked at the clock. He held up his hand to Mr Jay who was writing and said, 'Mr Nilsen. I am now going to charge you with the murder of Stephen Sinclair. Will you come this way, please?'

At 5.23 on the Friday, 47 hours and 53 minutes after he was arrested, Nilsen was taken in the ritualistic way to the charge room downstairs, behind the front office, where the accusation was read to him in the presence of other officers, seven minutes before the 48-hour deadline expired.

'You Dennis Nilsen, civil servant, aged thirty-seven years of 23 Cranley Gardens, Muswell Hill, in the County of London, are charged that you, on or about February the first this year, at the aforesaid address, did wilfully murder one Stephen Neil Sinclair of no fixed address with malice aforethought and against the Queen's Peace.'

Then followed the caution that he was not obliged to say anything at that stage, but if he wished so to do whatever he said would be written down and may be used in evidence. Nilsen did not want to say anything so he was taken back to his cell and told that the interview would be resumed on another day.

Not one conference, but several, for despite Nilsen's

40

co-operation neither Chambers nor Jay would boast that they knew very much about their prisoner. They knew his name, that he had been a soldier, a policeman and now a civil servant and that at the beginning of February, which was only eleven days old, he had invited a stranger called Sinclair back to his flat for a drink and had killed him. Unlike the other victims, of which the police wanted to hear much more, Nilsen had been unable to dispose of Sinclair's body.

True, Sinclair had been decapitated, his skull boiled and the rest of his corpse dismembered, but the multiple killer had not only been unable to separate the arms from the hands, but he had been unable to rid himself of the fingers which still bore the unmistakeable prints of the dead man. The fingerprints were also in the Criminal Records Office. But there was much more to the murder of Sinclair than that.

This was the murder investigation in reverse. The police had arrested the murderer first and were to find and hopefully identify the victims afterwards, so they set out to discover all they could about Nilsen before they tried to understand why he had killed Sinclair.

Some of the early truths about Nilsen emerged within hours of him being charged. From his home county, for instance, from a neat council house, 6 Bairn Road in the village of Strichen, just twelve miles by car from the nearest town of Fraserburgh, in north Aberdeenshire, and six hundred miles from London. Strichen is a village where existence is well ordered, placid, even content. Like the 'broch', as the general wider area of Buchan in that part of the county is known. It is timeless. The buildings mostly of Peterhead granite will last for ever. The countryside that sweeps down from the Grampians to the sea owes more to nature than to modern husbandry.

No one believed that anything could change until

the ill tidings reached Strichen with an impact that would take a long time to subside. Nilsen's mother, Mrs Elizabeth Duthie Scott, formerly Nilsen, nee Whyte, had little notice of the intelligence that was to sorely test the tranquillity of her life. Her eldest son, Olav, had called by telephone to say, 'Better sit down, Mum, I've something bad to tell you.'

What could she say to the news? Her son, a mass murderer?

The gossip, the questions, they all took her back to the time when she was a bonny lass, Elizabeth Duthie Whyte, the daughter of Andrew Whyte, a fisherman aboard the boats that plied for herring from the busy port of Fraserburgh, and of Lily Whyte, nee Duthie. Her father became a ship's engineer before he died, but mother was still living in the harbour town, in the rear flat upstairs at 47 Academy Road, one of a council block of four. Elizabeth had left school before the outbreak of the Second World War and was working in a draper's shop when the conflict sailed into port. It came in the shape of fishing smacks that needed protection against enemy aircraft, surface vessels and submarines, in the shape of warships that needed a safe haven for refuelling and re-provisioning, in the shape of escaping Allied vessels and their precious crews of fighting men and women and refugees from the Nazi war machine.

The war was seven months old when Adolf Hitler, on April 1, 1940, decided to invade Norway. The future of all able bodied Norwegians became perilous. Many remaining did not believe the invasion would materialize. When it did begin on April 9 the evacuation gained impetus. The Germans arrived by warships in Oslo and Stavanger as thousands headed for the minor fjords and other escape routes to Britain. The small Allied presence which had hoped to forge a link across

Norway with the industrial potential of Sweden had to withdraw.

When, on June 7, King Haakon and his government left Norway to spend the rest of the war in belligerent exile, the last of the Norwegians who could escape came with him. Olav Magnus Nilsen was one of them. A clerk in a tobacco factory, he was one of many who sailed in the smaller boats from the lesser Norwegian inlets to Fraserburgh, the nearest Allied port to the Norwegian coast. The tiny Scottish town, whose inhabitants today only number twelve thousand, became the assembly point, permanent camp and dispersal post for many Scandinavians who were to don uniform in the Allied cause.

Welcoming parties were organized by the churches, Salvation Army and Red Cross. With committees devoted to the knitting of comforts and raising money for the war effort, they held parties in aid of charity and even occasional dances. At one of these, Elizabeth Whyte met Olav, her dashing blond private now with the First Norwegian Brigade.

On Saturday, May 2, 1942, she became Mrs Nilsen at the Congregational Church in Fraserburgh. The Reverend John J. George who performed the marriage ceremony preached a brief homily on the dangers of sudden, quick wartime romances. These might not progress to the fulfilment required by the good Lord who had instituted marriage primarily for the purpose of the procreation of children. The Reverend George should not have worried. Olav, junior, was born the following year and still lives in Fraserburgh, in West Road, just a stone's throw from the home in Academy Road where grandmother Whyte still resides.

Three years later, on November 23, 1945, Dennis Andrew was born at Academy Road. He was born, as he explained later, under the sign of Sagittarius, the half man, half horse archer centaur of Greek mythology. Down to earth, he was named Andrew for his grand-father, Andrew Whyte, and for the patron saint of Scotland. Dennis, his first name, was a more difficult choice. It was not common or popular and was selected for fancy rather than reason. It was interchangeable with Denis or Denys, but Dennis complained, during the boredom of his prison days on remand awaiting trial, that *The Guardian* newspaper had spelled his name with a single 'n'. He was usually known to his friends as 'Desi'.

Two years after the arrival of Dennis, Mrs Nilsen gave birth to a daughter, Sylvia. Each of the children thrived and were originally the source of much pleasure to their mother. Her husband was not. In her straightforward Scots way she made no defence of her marriage to Private, later Sergeant, Olav Nilsen. He was a violent, drunken womaniser who was constantly absent from the family home. 'He did nothing for me. I had to bring up the children virtually single-handed. When he did come home he was as good as useless. He was no good to me at all,' she said bitterly.

Seven years after the marriage Mrs Nilsen obtained a divorce. Dennis had always been, from any practical point of view, fatherless. 'If he met his father in the street he would not have recognized him,' his mother declared.

In the absence of a father Dennis grew very attached to the grandfather whose name he bore, Andrew Whyte, even though the fisherman turned ship's engi-neer was often away at sea. When the old man returned to port he would spend every available moment with his favourite grandchild at their council flat, then at 73 Mid Street, Fraserburgh. And when he went to sea again, Dennis, even as a toddler, would wander out of

44

the front door and go down the street calling, 'Grandpa.'

The bond was short enough. When he was seven he was called from class at Fraserburgh Infants' School to be told that his grandfather had died at sea. The boy was to recall, in his later youth and early manhood, that he had no one to turn to for consolation. He would escape to a disused air raid shelter on nearby open ground seeking solace in the company of pigeons, which he watered and fed.

If he was inconsolable over the loss of his grandfather, he was devastated at what happened to his feathered friends. Someone went into the air raid shelter at night and slaughtered them. Adults tried to explain to the boy that the pigeons had canker, the dreaded disease which can decimate flocks of pigeons and which demands that pigeon fanciers put their birds down, usually by wringing their necks. As he had not slaughtered his own birds some local had done it for him. Otherwise they might have infected surrounding lofts.

To Dennis it seemed inexplicable. Someone had strangled his birds. No adult had admitted it. No youngster had been caught. And Dennis kept his silence and his solitude.

In 1954 Mrs Nilsen married again. She took the name Scott, the national family name of highlanders, from her marriage to Adam Scott, a county council roadman. He came from New Pitsligo, the village next to Strichen, where they set up their new home. Adam was eight years younger than Elizabeth and their marriage produced four more children, three sons and a daughter. With cousins and aunts it became a big family, so large in numbers that Dennis had to confide, from his prison cell, 'I didn't know I had so many relatives, more than I have friends.'

45

If, as some suspected, Dennis occupied Mrs Scott's mind more than the other six children she was too astute a mother to show it. 'He was always a bit of a loner,' she conceded. He found two attractions in his life: one was the uniforms of authority, notably those of the armed services; the other the creation of artistic works, particularly painting and poetry. At the village school he passed the standard examinations at an average level but won special prizes with his paintings and verse competition. His former head teacher, Miss Melita Lee, found him 'an average boy, a willing pupil. He just got on with anything you gave him, but he was better at art than scientific subjects and I always thought he would take up a career with an artistic bias.'

As for the attraction of uniforms, the Life Boys, the junior section of the Boys' Brigade, the Christian organization founded in Glasgow in 1883 by Sir William Smith, claimed his first allegiance, though he quickly tired of the modest adventure that it offered. He was, after all, born in the aftermath of war, six months after the conflict ended in Europe, and three months before the cessation of hostilities in the Far East. Still, and around him was the magnetism of war, tales of the return of heroes, the mourning of the fallen, the sound of air raid sirens, the thundering of low flying aircraft, and the sight of some crippled, shell-torn ship limping into Fraserburgh harbour.

The panoply of war left its mark even on those too young to remember actual fighting. All around him raged the argument whether there would ever be peace, real peace, whether Britain should disarm or rearm, whether to recruit more soldiers or demobilise the existing regular units. The old told him as he grew up, 'you are too young to remember'. Dennis's answer was to enlist in the Army Cadet Corps to learn parade-ground drill, fieldcraft and how to fire a gun.

Johnny Craig, the local postman, was his cadet commandant. To him Dennis was 'a loon', in Scots vernacular a rogue, scamp, a scarcely worthwhile person. Certainly, he thought, the young Nilsen would benefit from Army life and discipline. Dennis felt comfortable in the macho military world, and, as the forces were recruiting again, he pestered the non-commissioned officers at the Army Information Centre in Broad Street, in nearby Peterhead. He hung about the gates of the Bridge of Don barracks in the granite city of Aberdeen, the nearest 'capital' he knew. There he saw the pipes and drums and men of the Gordon Highlanders. He marvelled at their standards, battle honours and badges, from Corunna in Spain, Kandahar in India, the Somme of the First World War and El Alamein and Sicily in the Second. It thrilled the young observer. A Scot and a highlander he might have been but, alas, he was no kilt-swinging Jock and certainly no 'cocky wee Gordon, the pride of them a'.

Such regimental ambitions were not for him, yet he still sought a military career.

Mrs Scott tried to explain his shortcomings. 'He was not one for the girls. Come to think about it he didn't seek out the company of other boys either. He used to take his sister, Sylvia, to parties. She was the only girl I knew he took out. I didn't think there was anything unusual in that, you know. Any mother would take the notion that at fifteen, sixteen, seventeen there would be a suitable girl coming along for him soon. There was no hurry.'

Dennis, to her mind, was too much concerned with sculpting a career for himself. 'Everyone assumed he would take up a career in art, but one day he came back from school and said, "Mum, I want to join the

Army." And that's what he did. He became a boy soldier.' There was no march into battle for him. From the Army Cadet Corps he went to the Army, not with a rifle and a bayonet, but with a carving knife and fork, to Aldershot and the Royal Army Catering Corps. When mocked about his career he retorted, 'You said I was an artist and cooking is an art.'

If the famous recruiting poster had been adapted from the Royal Navy to read 'Join the Army and see the world' Nilsen could not have achieved a better travelling career. After training at Aldershot, the great Hampshire home of the British Army, he was posted in turn to cook for the Royal Fusiliers at Osnabruck in Lower Saxony, West Germany, for the Queen's Own Borderers in Aden, for the Trucial Scouts in Oman, for the Argyll and Sutherland Highlanders in Aden and for other regiments in Cyprus and Berlin.

While his army career was widely spread across the globe, his promotion prospects were remarkably poor. From the day he became an adult soldier in 1963 it took him two years to become a lance corporal, and another year to become a corporal, the highest rank he achieved. His Army record shows that he was frequently in skirmishes of one kind or another, usually associated with drink. Not long after he was posted to West Germany he became involved in a marathon lunch-time drinking session, first in the Naafi and then in the barrack room, during which there was an argument in which Dennis was beaten up and had to have treatment from the army medical officer.

No one took much professional notice at the time but some behavioural and mental facets of Dennis's make up were revealed on his first overseas posting. In the British Army of the Rhine he became fanatical about cooking, became rapidly addicted to alcohol and secretive about his relationships with other people.

48

One fellow private, Michael Procopis, born in London of Greek parents and now living in Toronto, Canada, remembers that 'he wanted to be the best chef he could be, the best in the Army. He didn't talk about his family life, the folks back home, the place where he grew up, went to school and to work. Unlike most soldiers when they are away from home he said nothing about them.

'But there were few people who knew more about cooking than he did and there was certainly nobody who could butcher a pig, cook it and present it like he did and he made sure you knew it.'

Procopis once posed with him for a photograph. They were both in chef's fatigues, standing by a pig, complete with lemon in the mouth and parsley behind the ears, ready for the officers' mess party. 'The officers knew a good cook when they saw one and they insisted that he should always prepare the food for their big functions.'

Nilsen's predilection for the culinary arts gave him another peculiarity. 'He had this very odd thing about carving knives,' said Procopis. Knives, forks, spoons are always in plentiful supply in the army and cooking utensils are issued at will to cooks, but when it came to knives Nilsen regarded them as his own very personal, private property, more like a Bible, a razor or a face flannel, something that is never given or lent to anyone else. He would let nobody else touch them and kept them in a special folding wallet of reinforced cloth. There was a cleaver, a carving knife, a serrated edged meat knife, a paring knife, a butcher's knife, a bread knife and more. No one had as many knives as he did.

'I thought it strange at the time,' Procopis continued. 'He knew all there was to know about knives, and he kept talking about them, what kind of steel is the strongest, which kind of knife is the most reliable for making certain cuts, which is the sharpest and which can be ground to the best edge. I put it down to the fact that he wanted to be the very best chef he could be, but now I am not so sure.'

In time they would discover what Procopis knew, and that was Nilsen's dedication to drink. On his nights off he would imbibe large quantities of vodka, neat vodka. He would become monumentally alcoholised. As Procopis recalls, 'One night he came back to the barracks very drunk. When he went to sleep we tied him to his bed by the wrists and the ankles and took him and the bed out into the pouring rain and left him there. When he came to he brought his bed and sodden bedding back into the barracks but he didn't say a word about it. He didn't complain. He didn't explain. That was him.'

On another occasion he came back to his billet from a night out without any trousers, and perhaps more understandably he did not talk about that either. He may have been in trouble, but, in the eyes of his buddies, he would always take the easy way out. He was no fighter. At the same time he had a quick, violent temper. He would suddenly flare like a lucifer, but whatever the dispute, no matter how serious, it would quickly fizzle out. Like the time he had an argument with another squaddy about cooking. The dispute ended with the trading of punches, but it was a one-way transaction and Nilsen suffered the worst of it.

The combination of loneliness, secrecy about his family, and his capacity for drinking copious quantities of vodka isolated Nilsen from his fellows. 'He could pack it away,' was how his barrack mates recalled his consumption of distilled rye, but he had to be left very much alone after such sessions because he was physically helpless and incomprehensible.

Sober, or at the start of a drinking bout, he was a great talker, but those who listened to him found that he tended to dwell on one subject giving the impression that he was recently exhaustively rather than well read on the matter. Book educated, his brain soaked up the facts as his stomach absorbed alcohol. What he learned was passed on to others in a deluge of words against which the listener could neither add a point of view nor interrupt with a correction.

Nilsen would argue, ignoring how right or wrong his case, and if he looked like being thwarted in reason or fact he would fall back on the defence, 'We're not on the same wavelength,' a ploy he used on his own mother as well as his army colleagues.

Few of them had either the time or the inclination to analyse their comrade for his qualities or his shortcomings, but they noticed that in troubled times during his service he sought comfort in writing home. This was very true when he was in Aden, where the British wanted the old colonial territory to merge into a South Arabian Federation to make a bigger, better economic base, or so they said. Communist-backed nationalists resisted the measure and fought the British in the narrow alleys of straw-reinforced, sun-baked mud brick huts.

At such times Nilsen would retire to his bunk, pull out his note pad and write home. His mother remembered the letters 'when the Arabs rioted at the El-Mansoura prison, the kind of time when the trouble was all over the newspapers. He wrote a lot then.' She interpreted it as a reaction of a good son who wanted to allay his mother's fears. That is the way she saw it, what she told those around her, and no one would persuade her that it was because her son was frightened or even insecure.

To her he remained 'the gentle, caring boy he was

51

and always will be. Why, he once came home with a little bird with a broken wing and asked for a shoe box to put it in to look after it.'

This was a compassion that he did not, as far as his fellow soldiers could discover, share with any other living creatures. It was his inability to find common ground with others which increasingly isolated him from his fellow men. It also told against him when, after ten years' service, he could not really expect to be promoted to the rank of sergeant.

Because of his drinking habits he was lucky not to have been charged and disciplined and even reduced to the ranks. Remarkably, the only time he appeared on a charge was in his last year of service, 1972, when in the stricter barrack discipline of the United Kingdom, even in the Shetland Islands, he was charged with entertaining civilians on Army premises without authority at 1.40 a.m. and was sentenced to be reprimanded. That incident was on April 30. Seven months later he decided he had had enough of soldiering. He had served ten years, first as a boy soldier then as an adult regular. Now he declined to sign on for another period of service and returned home to Strichen with the boasts expected of the much-travelled serviceman.

One of his claims was that he had been cooking for the Queen while she was on holiday with the royal family at Balmoral, their seat on Deeside. Truth of the matter was that, like so many cooks before him, he was posted to cater for other soldiers. This posting was to Ballater to prepare food for the guards who would go to Balmoral to protect the Queen. Ballater was ten miles away, and that was the closest he came to meeting the sovereign.

Mrs Scott smiled at the recollection. 'When he was in the Army he would come home on leave and get the other boys down to the village shops to get all the spices to cook something special. But I was always left with the dishes to wash. "Chefs don't do that," he used to explain. He was a rascal.

'And he would tell us all his stories. I always remember him saying he went into a restaurant and called out, "Garçon!" When the waiter came up Dennis asked him if he had any frogs' legs. When the waiter said, "Yes," Dennis told him to "Hop out and get me some beer then."

'When he came out of the Army he was popular with the young ones. They loved his stories and he used to enjoy showing them how good a cook he really was, preparing them special treats, and he was particularly good at decorating the salmon.'

Dennis seemed at first content to return to Civvy Street, but he had not calculated on the strictures of Strichen and Fraserburgh. They were essentially very small places, the village and the port, the kind of places where residents gossip for hours on the telephone when they have obtained a wrong number. Beyond the gossip there was herring to catch and very little else. Work was not plentiful, not even for chefs who were good at their trade.

The former army chef, having shed his uniform and fatigues, cast off the burdens of small Scottish town restrictions. After only a few weeks at home he left for London and at least one member of the family thought it might be the last they would see or hear of him.

A fierce family quarrel had erupted during his brief stay. Olav, his elder brother, an engineer, married with two young children, had good reason to be unimpressed by Dennis. The younger brother did not keep in regular touch with his mother or the family, nor did he contribute to her modest income, even when he had money. He drank too much and he was, to say the very least, 'a little bit odd'.

Even ten years later when Nilsen was in a prison cell, and much in need of family feeling and comfort, the battle lingered and the rift remained. 'We had a row over something silly which reached much bigger proportions,' Olav recounted. 'I told him to apologize, but he didn't. So I told him not to come back to my house until he decided to say that he was sorry.' From that day in 1974 neither Olav, his wife Trudy, nor their children saw Dennis again.

'I always felt sure that Dennis wasn't certain of himself. Once he seemed to want to get himself sorted out. But then he went into the army. When he came out he was in his late twenties and he hadn't changed. He had got worse. I thought he would come out a man at last, but he was a long way short of that. He couldn't talk about his problems. He never confided in anybody and never admitted anything. To hide his failures he became arrogant, rude and offensive.' Olav made up his mind that his brother was a homosexual, and it angered him. Why could his brother not be a normal male, husband and father of two children? Not that Olav was the first to notice by any means, even though Dennis would not discuss human affinity at any level. He was a misogynist, whose 'gentle, caring nature' had developed into an agonized personality complex. Secretive, lonely, he liked to give the impression of being an aesthete. The years in which his tender hands created artistic works, from line-drawn flowers, and water-coloured ships to dressing salmon had all but gone. He feared or knew, although he would never admit it, that the artistic talents recognized by his teachers had waned.

His tall, slim almost frail physique had not entirely disappeared as a result of army diet and discipline, and he still seemed to enquiring minds mentally bright but physically wanting. Physically he withdrew from

54

encounters and challenges; mentally he always seemed to be weighing up whether an acquaintance was his intellectual superior or inferior. Once he knew he would out-talk the other party to prove, at least to himself, that he was superior.

Since he was not often able to impress those about him, particularly in the army, he had to rely on his one life-long supporter, his mother, at moments of triumph and disaster. Just as he had written to her when there was trouble around him in the army, so he corresponded when he achieved anything. Like becoming a property guard at the Department of the Environment in Marsham Street, Westminster, where the address was impressive, if the rank lowly.

Like the time he became a policeman. In his search for work he called at the careers information office of the Metropolitan Police in Victoria Street and was referred to the recruiting office at Harrow Road and accepted. First he had to undergo a medical test which he passed. He did not have the necessary four Ordinary or two Advanced level certificates in the General Certificate of Education, but he could boast that in the Army he had passed the Education Corps certificates in mathematics, English, civic affairs, catering, science and military history. A kindly senior officer waived the requirement, telling him, 'A lot of our recruits have no formal academic qualifications, but develop their fuller potential in later life. It has been proved that if you pass our tests you will probably have no difficulty in making the grade later on.'

Dennis succeeded in both the written test and even in the 'full, frank and confidential' discussion during which he was expected to answer a considerable number of personal and family questions. They included why he wanted to join the police. To which he gave one of those bland answers so beloved by public officials which sound so banal to those outside the public service. 'I feel it is my duty to use what talents I have for the benefit of the public at large,' said Nilsen and he was almost 'in'. They sent him away while they checked out his personal and family history and he survived the scrutiny.

When the Commissioner for the Metropolitan Police, Sir Kenneth Newman, demanded to know why someone like Nilsen had been admitted to his service all the relevant papers concerning his recruitment had vanished.

When Nilsen reported back to Peel House, the training centre at Hendon, Middlesex, after his background had supposedly been vetted he took the formal declaration that:

'I do solemnly and sincerely declare and affirm that I will well and truly serve our Sovereign Lady the Queen in the Office of Constable, without fear or affection, malice or ill will; and that I will, to the best of my power, cause the peace to be kept and preserved, and prevent all offences against the persons and properties of Her Majesty's subjects and that while I continue to hold the said office I will, to be best of my skill and knowledge, discharge all the duties thereof faithfully according to the law.'

Mrs Scott was so proud of her second born. She carried his letter about with her for a very long time, showing it to people she met in the shops and at the post office in Strichen. He had been accepted as a probationary policeman.

This involved him moving into a single room provided in the Peel House centre training school at Hendon, where he began to study government and law, society and the police, the powers of arrest, how to uphold traffic regulations, treat illnesses and deal with accidents, how to investigate theft, hold the balance between citizens in civil disputes and particularly how to deal with juvenile delinquency.

Court procedure, communications and police regulations were the subjects of the lessons that followed. Dennis did well enough, and, if his colleagues of the time are to be believed, he worked hard and excelled in courses on 'assaults: what are they, how serious, and how to get the facts and collect evidence' and on 'murder and robbery: what to do and what not to do when called to the scene of a suspicious death or robbery before the Criminal Investigation Department get there'.

It was excellent training for a mass murderer.

After fifteen weeks training at Peel House, Nilsen was ready for the next step, to go to one of London's one hundred and eighty police stations, and in the company of an old sweat, or 'experienced home beat officer' as they prefer to be called, to patrol the streets. He was posted to Willesden Green.

While waiting for his probationary rank and posting as Police Constable Nilsen, D.A., 287 Q-for-Queen Division and his police warrant card No. 164305, he took a short leave in his Aberdeenshire homeland, and got into trouble. Even police training had not curbed his temper. If anything the authority his police badge gave him made him feel more secure in any argument. One night at the Station Hotel, Fraserburgh, at a potato merchants' dinner, he got the worst of an argument and was seen shouting one moment and lying on the floor, his face covered in blood, the next.

All the qualities and defects that had been noticed by his army buddies were now seen by his fellow constables as the loner went about his work. When he talked it was non-stop about the papers he had studied at Peel House. He did not get on. It may be that he realized that he could not succeed in physical encounters with drunks or criminals, make arrests, or even talk people out of their civil disputes. His own excuse was that the money was not good enough, for the Edmund Davies report which resulted in considerable pay rises for the police (in exchange for a permanent agreement never to strike) had not yet been made.

Fortunately for the police Nilsen decided that he was not suitable material to be a policeman and after eleven months and three weeks he handed in his papers – the technical form of resignation – gave back most of his uniform and returned to civilian life.

An ordinary job in the competitive world of commerce and industry was not for Dennis. He chose to remain securely on the payroll of the country. He had been a soldier, a policeman and now he would be a civil servant, starting as usual at the ground floor – of the Department of the Environment, in Marsham Street, Westminster, as a property guard. It was not exactly in the civil service, the work being carried out by contractors, but he liked the address even if the rank was lowly.

Very soon he was able to write to his mother with news of a step up the civil service ladder. 'Dear Mum,' he began, 'Giving you the usual excuses for not having written sooner. They say that opportunity never knocks twice so I've taken advantage of an enterprising offer to advance my position by becoming a civil servant. (Being now older and maturer to take up such a post). I am now an employment officer with the MANPOWER SERVICES COMMISSION (EMPLOYMENT SERVICES AGENCY) formally (sic) in the Dept of Employment. (Better pay and conditions than in the long suffering fuzz).

'I have acquired a very intimate circle of friends in

town and feel that any other place would be a poor substitute for good old LONDON.

'The only major disadvantages of living in the city is that the general rate of inflation seems to be higher here. The costliest unit being accommodation i.e. £80 p.w.

'A good friend of mine has been trying to persuade me to become an Assistant Cameraman (film). Colin is a film director who makes 50 min. documentaries for OMNIBUS. His latest effort is one on the life of the ballet dancer NIJINSKY (to be screened this winter. B.B.C.).

'I work in our office in DENMARK ST WC1 just off OXFORD ST. It's a 9–5 MON–FRI. It's good to get up in the morning put a suit on and do a satisfying clean job. I mainly interview people for managerial and general vacancies in the HOTEL and CATERING INDUSTRY. Our boss is Michael Foot Sec. of State for Employment. I am also involved with compiling statistics for the GOVT'S monthly figures. (Suitably doctored to create a favourable impression). I would return to the MET police tomorrow if the pay was increased and general conditions improved.'

Mrs Scott was proud of her son. The Commission was set up to help people train for jobs and obtain employment which satisfies their aspirations and abilities and helps employers find suitable workers. Dennis so impressed his superiors that he was promoted to executive officer and he sent his mother a photograph of himself seated behind his desk, the model always allocated to officers of that rank, double pedestal, six drawer. At last he felt he was somebody. As he added in his letter, 'I am involved in work assisting homeless people.'

'So like Dennis,' said Mrs Scott: 'Always doing something that will help other people.'

It was some years before she was to learn that the 'gentle, caring person' helped those people to a drink, to sleep and to their deaths. He found some of them through the Job Centres, first at Denmark Street and later at Kentish Town Road, joined them in pubs and then took them home, first to Melrose Avenue and then to Cranley Gardens where he killed them. When Mrs Scott did hear the news she said, 'I never imagined anything about him could be so bad. I just don't understand it. Not from a boy of mine. It seems Dennis has done these things,' and lapsing for a moment into her 'broch' dialect, 'I canna discard my son.'

Some friends and neighbours, the dour, private and ashamed, thought she should have shut her door and stayed inside with her sorrow instead of telling the world about him, but that was not her way. 'I've always believed in God. My parents were very strict Christians. We couldn't even do any clothes washing on Sundays. But I've never been a regular churchgoer. So when all this blew up I just prayed to God for strength to cope with it and to help Dennis cope with it as well. And do you know? God has helped me, for I am managing somehow to cope in spite of the enormity of what Dennis did. And I know from his letters that Dennis is coping as well.'

Dennis was again protecting his mother from the truths about life in prison. She stood by him even though he had never been a devoted son, had never – by her own account – ever said, 'Here's a pound, Mum,' even when he was earning good money. 'Still, all I can do for Dennis is to give him moral support from a distance. I hope he remains sensible and co-operates and does things properly from now on. I am heartily sorry for the people who have been hurt, the families of these boys . . .' She hesitated, trying to pronounce the letter 'v' and the word 'victims', but it would not come. Through her tears she said, 'I am sorry for the families of these boys, whoever they were. You know a mother cannot store all her natural feelings for only her own flesh and blood. She must have some for the rest of human people, whoever they are.'

As she spoke, her sixty-fourth birthday occurred, but there was no letter from her son, no card. 'When he didn't used to write when he was in the army or away in London I would sometimes have a wee bit weep and then I would say to myself, "he's so busy," and I would sit down and write to him.' So, on her birthday, she sat down and wrote to her son in Brixton Prison, to comfort him. She had tried to tell him gently that she stood by him without being able to say how or why, without letting him know that she was so ashamed that he was both a homosexual and a mass murderer.

Meanwhile, his grandmother, Mrs Lily Whyte, at the age of eighty-six, when told the news at the old home in Academy Road, Fraserburgh, said, 'It must have all been in self defence.' When told there were several bodies she replied, 'The poor boy is sick. He needs medical help.'

Five

Death, the leveller, shares its tragedies, particularly in the case of murder. It brought catastrophe to the Nilsen family, and grief to the adoptive family of victim Stephen Sinclair.

The Nilsen family did not understand Dennis. The Sinclair family could not humanly protect Stephen.

Stephen Neil No Name was born in 1962, the son of an unmarried mother from Perth, the ancient Scots city at the foot of Kinnoul Hill on the banks of the River Tay. He was not the only epileptic child born out of wedlock to the same epileptic mother, who later married and had other children by her lawful husband. Stephen, being illegitimate, was – as so often happens in such areas – put into the care of the local authority, the former Perthshire County Council.

When he was fourteen months old the council decided to place him with foster parents. Fostering is sometimes known as 'pass the parcel' after the party game and that is not unjustified. In the game the person holding the parcel when the music stops suffers some forfeit or penalty. The same goes for parents who take in a foster child who turns out to be less than one hundred per cent physically or mentally normal.

Neil Sinclair, a retired army officer, and his wife, Elizabeth, a needlework teacher, knew nothing of Stephen's history when they took him in as a foster child, nor when they legally adopted him a few months later and gave him their name. They had three daughters, yearned for a son, and loved Stephen from the first time they saw him in 1963. He had that 'wonderful look of innocence and golden red hair, not carroty but really golden,' said Mrs Sinclair.

There was nothing apparently amiss with him except a squint. It was ordinary enough and the defect was treated until the strabismus disappeared. What the parents did not know was that by nature Stephen was a misfit. He returned love and kindness with disinterest, discipline with rebellion, and he became in time both anti-social and lawless.

For a long time he could control neither his bladder nor his bowels. He gave his early teachers no indication that he would achieve anything in scholastic or sporting terms. His school record of truancy and lack of application became so abysmal that both social and medical advice was sought. Well-meaning child guidance 'experts' suggested the abandonment of all discipline. Doctors diagnosed *petit mal* but he was later discovered to be an epileptic.

This psycho-motor epilepsy demanded his removal from home. He was admitted to the Royal Dundee Liff Hospital which caters for six hundred mental patients. And there he remained until he was twelve years old, beyond which time the institution could not cater for him. It was a blow to the Sinclairs.

They visited him regularly, supplied him with comforts but the hospital could not keep him and he was sent home as difficult and retarded as before. The stay at Liff merely limited his freedom to do himself and others harm. It did not cure him and he returned to the Sinclair bungalow home in the village of St Martin's, on the edge of Belbeggie, six miles north of Perth, with little or no promise of being integrated into the family circle with either happiness or security.

After Stephen's adoption, Mrs Sinclair had given birth to another two daughters, making five in all. In that environment, particularly after Stephen's return from Liff, he became increasingly the subject of parental attention. At the same time he had graduated from arsonist to a thief.

At the age of eight, he had attempted to set fire to the Sinclair home. 'I found him screwing up pages of the *Dundee Courier*, setting light to them and watching them drift through a hatch in the floor with what looked suspiciously like pleasure,' said silver haired Mrs Sinclair. 'If I had not smelled burning the house would have been burned to the ground.'

As Stephen went through his teenage years he was in and out of special schools, 'D'-grade schools for the educationally sub-normal, residential establishments, remand centres, Borstals and prisons. Reports from penal institutions showed that although he was given training he showed no aptitude for any of the skills on offer and could eventually hope only for unskilled work and that would have to be carried out under supervision.

There was no sign of improvement even in his last year at school. Returning from one remand centre he was sent, by some educational and administrative quirk, to the only place that could be found – a grammar school. He was totally unsuited to the environment. He started by calling out the fire brigade to a non-existent blaze. He embarked on an adventure of theft. He was entrusted with the school keys by the headmaster and he promptly flung them away in a field causing maximum inconvenience.

'Like so many of his escapades it had no reason,' said Mr Sinclair. 'It gained him nothing and caused others a lot of trouble. There was no sense in him. He had become silly and purposeless.'

Mr Sinclair tried to find him work, first in a field picking berries. On the first day he was dismissed for unruly behaviour. A post in a garage showed no improvement. He cheated the customers over prices and change and then robbed the safe. There was no doubt of his guilt and he was arrested and punished.

When Stephen came out of prison on one occasion he went to the Department of Health and Social Security in Mill Road to draw assistance money. At once he discovered where they kept his records and where the money was secured. That night he broke in, stole cash and set fire to documents containing his personal history. On the way out, with his customary foolishness, he scrawled some graffitti on the office wall that included his own National Insurance number. Police promptly arrested him again, took him to court, secured a conviction and saw him back into prison.

The daughters of Mr and Mrs Sinclair complained that Stephen was always the centre of attention. It was Stephen this and Stephen that, for ever demanding and being given attention and time. On one occasion the boy slashed his wrists in a markedly unsuccessful suicide bid. On another he threatened one of his sisters, a threat of violence which unlike previous menaces could not be ignored. The Sinclairs, exhausted, frustrated by their endless discussions and arguments with the so-called experts of authority, admitted defeat. They decided to renounce Stephen.

They told the local authority that they wished to return their adopted son to the care of the council, refusing all further responsibility. County hall officials were amazed. No one had ever tried to de-adopt a child before. They said it could not be done and threatened to take the Sinclairs to court to prove it. That incensed Mr Sinclair. He pointed out with great reluctance that in that case he would be compelled to make public the actions of the authority in fostering out a child, permitting it to be adopted, when there was ample reason to suspect or know that it came of an epileptic parentage.

It was no victory for the Sinclairs, merely the preservation of the family of mother, father and five daughters. Stephen was fostered out again, this time with a Perth family who had a number of girls in their care. He repaid their kindness by robbing them of all their money on the first day, buying a bottle of vodka and being found hopelessly drunk in the street.

'He was all take and no give,' Mr Sinclair said afterwards. 'If you gave him a cigarette he would smoke it. If someone gave him marijuana he would smoke it, vodka, he would drink it, glue or cocaine, he would sniff it. He was into everything that was free. He would take everything and give nothing.'

Stephen Neil Sinclair drifted, little more than a vagrant, rarely washing, going through skinhead and punk phases, growing his hair long, then having it cut in Mohican style, then shaved again depending on how the fashion or his street associates decided. They were a motley band of drug addicts, drunks, male prostitutes and fellow drifters. They said they liked Stephen because he would 'go along with anything.'

When in Perth, free from any parental, adoptive or foster, care or control he spent his time looking up old acquaintances from remand centres, Borstal and prison with whom he could exchange boasts about his wrong-doing, information on where to get food, money and lodging for nothing, and indulge in any current vice. A favourite haunt was the Norie Miller Riverside Park in Perth, a veritable glue sniffers' paradise and worse. Stephen would while away his evenings there, often staying all night in warm weather.

It was an ideal innocent-looking haunt of tourists and lovers and an open Mecca to drug pushers, from pot or marijuana to smack or junk, the drug words for heroin. To the pushers Sinclair would be a pushover, an easy, gullible customer.

Much of the heroin sold on the smaller black markets of Britain, which together make up much of the illicit narcotic trade, is diluted and weakened by harmless powders like boracic or other ordinary chemist's shop preparations, and sold at no bargain price either. Stephen was no match for such uncrupulous people and as his friends seemed to dwindle with his hopes of any work or future he drifted away from the Tayside town.

The last member of the Sinclair family to see him was a married daughter, Valerie, who spotted him in a Perth street in 1982. They exchanged greetings. The conversation was as natural as could be expected from a drug addicted vagrant but she asked him about himself, his future, and he left her resigned to the thought that Stephen would always be a vagrant, always get by somehow, hopefully without hurting himself or others.

Stephen drifted to London which compared with Perth is an inhospitable hell, particularly for those without money, work or hope of employment. Yet the capital is still the magnet which attracts derelicts. They seek to survive without identity, lost among the large anonymous section of the population where they can, consciously or not, live on the fat of others without being identified, pilloried or punished.

In 1980, the most recent calculable year, there were 7,177 people missing in the United Kingdom. Scotland Yard's 'active' missing persons index for that and subsequent years hovers around the five thousand mark. In 1982 it listed 4,975 new names, half male, half female. Although the majority returned home safely, with their own excuses and justifications, there were still 236 males missing on the last day of the year.

When police, for one reason or another, cannot or will not activate a hunt for a missing person the task is often undertaken by the Salvation Army, which claims an eighty per cent success rate. The Army's investigation department knows, in the words of its chief, Colonel Bramwell Pratt, that 'if someone is determined to disappear into the vastness of London it is quite easy for him to do so. Of course when we let a bed for the night – and we let ten thousand places every night – we ask for the names of the occupants, but it is quite easy for them to give false information, false identities and it is virtually impossible to check the truth of them. We often have no reason whatsoever to make any check because in so many cases the family does not know or does not care that the person is missing. And if anything untoward happens to him nobody knows what to do because nobody has any idea who that person may be.'

That was Stephen Sinclair.

Those who have not the voice or the cash, like Sinclair, have to seek out their food, friends and lodging more desperately. They tend to stray to places like 'Cardboard City', that area on the pavements and in the alleys under and around the arches of the Charing Cross railway terminus where packing cases provide the only warmth from the weather and rare charities like the Silver Lady canteen provide tea and food.

The Salvation Army's success rate in looking for some five thousand wanderers a year is believed to rest mostly on the middle age bracket, between thirty and sixty, when men become introspective, look at themselves and question their purpose and future in life. They know their capabilities and fear their ambitions will lead them to failure. They feel they are imprisoned by circumstances, resentful and hating the life they have come to lead. They believe that if they disappear, run away, even take a new identity their fortunes in happiness and cash will improve.

Because deviating from the usual daily round of tasks is not natural to them they are more easily traced. That is not true of the large majority of missing persons, the teenagers and newly adult males. They can take temporary shelter with acquaintances which may result in permanent friendships or which lead to compromise and often, as in the case of Stephen Sinclair, tragedy.

He had exhausted the number of places where handouts are available. Salvation Army, Mungo Trust, the benevolent Scottish corporation, various social security offices had seen him come and go. One Scots acquaintance saw him in Denmark Street where Nilsen worked until 1982, where the early morning work seekers are hired as day to day kitchen staff by hotels and restaurants. 'Stephen could no' pick up his feet let alone a wiper to do the dishes,' he recalled. All that was left for Stephen to do was to sell his body as a male prostitute. If the acquaintance was to be believed Stephen had no money, no work, no prospects. He had lost weight, looked like a candidate for a hospital ward. Wherever he sought help he was advised to look for more permanent work. Try a Job Centre, they said. He had tried Denmark Street, but the work was too heavy for him. Now he was directed to the Centre at 178 Kentish Town Road where some kindly official recommended him to a nearby hostel. Sinclair was in trouble immediately for stealing from a fellow resident at the hostel, arrested, brought before magistrates at Highbury Corner and remanded on his own recognizances to appear in a week's time.

In that week, the last in January, he again met Nilsen, whom he remembered from Denmark Street, Soho

pubs and the Kentish Town Road Job Centre ...
Coincidence? Or was it like the night he spoke to
Stuart Coles, thirty-six years of age, a Welsh labourer,
living ten doors from Nilsen in Melrose Avenue? One
night after reviewing his prospects of finding work
over a few pints of beer in a pub, Coles weaved his
way homewards by a route 266 bus to Willesden Green
and then via Riffel Road to Melrose Avenue. Behind
him came a stranger with a dog, Nilsen with Bleep.

'Hello,' he said affably. 'You're Taffy Coles, aren't
you?'

Coles agreed but was puzzled how the stranger knew
him.   •

Nilsen told him, 'You're out of work, aren't you?'

'I am indeed,' said Coles.

Nilsen explained that he was with the Manpower
Services Commission and might be able to help him.
If Coles would like to accompany him to 195 Melrose
Avenue he would give the unemployed labourer a
telephone number that he could call which might result
in him finding work.

Coles, swollen with alcohol and with a bladder
which needed evacuating, agreed. Nilsen opened the
front door of the house but kept him in the hall. He
offered the stranger a drink, but regretted he did not
have any beer. All he had, he said, was orange juice, so
Coles, hopping from one foot to another in anticipation
of finding a lavatory, took the drink and put it down
untasted.

'I noticed the place seemed to be unbearably hot,'
said Coles later. 'He was gone such a long time that I
went out of the house at the back and pee'd up against
the wall. I hadn't finished when this fellow comes
round yelling at me. "If I find you doing that again I'll
kill you," he screamed at me. I gave him a bit of verbal
back.

'I never got the telephone number. I never drank the orange juice if that's what it was. And when I saw him in the street he either ignored me or looked daggers at me. I still wonder how he knew about me, my name, that I lived in the same street, was a labourer and out of work. I suppose I can count myself very lucky . . .'

Luckier than Stephen Sinclair, the occasional prostitute and unemployable young man in search of work and shelter who met Nilsen. He went to Nilsen's subsequent home at Cranley Gardens. He never answered to his bail at Highbury Corner magistrates' court. He was never seen again. Alive. The next time he was brought to anyone's attention was when Nilsen told the detectives that he had killed Sinclair, and when other detectives rolled a severed finger on to an ink pad and a piece of paper, and an officer from the fingerprint branch of Scotland Yard said the print belonged to Stephen Neil Sinclair, aged twenty, convicted of offences . . .

Nilsen had not had time to dispose of Sinclair's body, so apart from the fingerprint record there was a boiled skull and other remains and the victim's last legacy, the hepatitis which could have killed him naturally as well as others. Tragic though it was it did not shock the Sinclairs when the police came to the door – as they had many times before – about Stephen. They asked the former adoptive parents if they had seen the news on television and added, 'a man has been charged with his murder.'

Mr Sinclair, his wife and family were distressed rather than surprised for they had suffered the anti-social life of Stephen and his friends, they had tried to correct it, and were hurt by the wagging tongues in the small communities of St Martin's and Belbeggie. Mr Sinclair could show that he had done more than could be expected for Stephen and threatened that he would sue to protect his wife, family and their good name.

He thought the local authority might be the best source of information on the crippled life and horrendous end of Stephen. 'We can only hope that times have changed and this could not occur again.'

Six

If a man talks a lot eventually he will be believed. That is an old saying but it was very true of Dennis Nilsen. Even though he accurately identified Stephen Sinclair as his last murder victim and went on to name others, the detectives, Chambers and Jay, found themselves increasingly pierced by the shafts of disbelief. He was so quietly spoken, so matter of fact. He neither bragged nor apologized for snuffing out the lives of so many people.

Undramatic, unmoved by his horrendous deeds, he treated the extraordinary story of carnage as a mere catalogue of commonplace events. So much so that the listeners became more prone to doubt than policemen usually are.

They found that the instrument of murder, the ligature, was the same but the selection of victims and the motive or motives incomprehensible. Particularly when he told how he killed a young man called Ken. He could not remember the surname, but the police had good reason eventually to recognize the description and details the dead man, even though they had, in his case, neither corpse nor fragments by which he could be physically identified.

Kenneth Ockenden was so unlike Stephen Sinclair. While Sinclair was an unemployed drifter and vagrant, Ockenden was a hard-working emigrant to Canada and when last seen was enjoying a long-planned holiday in Britain. While the Scot might have begged for shelter the Canadian already had a temporary accommodation. Both sought company but that was hardly a satisfactory explanation as to why they should both lose their lives at the hands of the strangler.

Kenneth and his parents, Ken, senior, and Audrey Ockenden, came originally from Croydon, Surrey. They lived at 16 Westbury Road and on February 9, 1956, Kenneth James was born to Audrey at St Mary's Maternity Hospital in St James's Road. Kenneth went to school nearby until he was fourteen when the family emigrated to the great dominion. They chose Burlington on the eastern shore of Lake Ontario, closer to the county seat of Hamilton than Toronto, the capital city of the province of Ontario on the northern shore. Ken, senior, took a job as a janitor with the nearby Halton Board of Education, and the family settled down to build a new life in Raldolph Crescent. Son Kenneth went to a technical college near Toronto, learned to be a welder, and with the money he earned at that trade saved for a holiday in the mother country.

Three months of visiting relatives, old school chums and seeing parts of Britain he had missed as a child was his ambition and in September, 1979, he flew into Heathrow. He looked young for his twenty-three years, his dark shoulder-length hair hanging like a Gothic arch round his clean, clear-featured face. In no way was he a problem boy, a wayward youth or a foolhardy young man. A quiet, neat and in some ways precise young fellow he smoked and drank in moderation, enjoyed photography and listening to rock music. He had grown up in the security of a happy home and there was no reason for him to vanish.

His holiday planning went according to schedule. There was more than enough money. No one need worry. He had kept in touch with his parents by telephone and letter, visited all the friends and relatives on his list and maintained constant contact with his mother's brother, Uncle Gordon Gillies. Then Kenneth disappeared without trace.

On Monday, December 3, 1979, a damp, overcast day, he reserved a room for the night at an hotel in King's Cross, paying for a further night in advance. He had breakfast and went out between 9 and 10 a.m., leaving behind most of his personal property including a diary which was to help police chart every day of his travels through England during his three month stay. Every day, that is, until December 3.

At about three o'clock in the afternoon of that day he telephoned Uncle Gordon at Carshalton and told him, 'I'm going home for Christmas, Uncle, so I'll come over on Wednesday and collect the money you're keeping for my return fare, if that's all right.'

Wednesday would be December 5, a day and a half away. Of course it was all right. Uncle Gordon had the thousand Canadian dollars in safe keeping. He told Ken that he looked forward to seeing him and hearing about his travels. But his nephew never came and the money was never collected. At first Mr Gillies thought he might have changed his mind but when he did not call by Christmas and his parents wondered why he had not been in touch the police were told.

The police were interested for he was not just any missing person, not someone who could have been suspected of vanishing deliberately. All the diary evidence left behind in the hotel room proved to the contrary. As did the conversation with his uncle.

Police looked for him, for his British Passport, number C543388A, issued by the British High Commission in Ottawa, his Ontario driver's licence, number 01618-43155-60209. They wanted to know what had happened to the valuable camera equipment he was carrying, a canon single lens reflex with the serial number 315448TX, a lens (1210427 FD 50-F 18) and a telephoto lens (171431 FD 28-F28). And they searched in vain despite the fact that, unlike so many of Nilsen's victims, his immediate history and movements were documented and traceable.

In February, 1980, two months after his disappearance, his parents flew into London to help police with the search. 'We are staying here as long as it takes to find Ken,' said his distraught mother.

Police were convinced that he had been the victim of foul play. Detective Inspector Roy Davies explained, 'He did not arrive at his uncle's to collect his fare. He has never been seen or heard of again and there is no explanation for his disappearance. He literally disappeared without trace. The very close family ties he maintained were broken, seemingly forever, on that day, December 3, for no natural reason.

'Circumstantially, all the evidence points to Ken Ockenden being dead. No body or other trace apart from his personal belongings in his hotel room has ever been found, despite joint enquiries by both officers of the Metropolitan Police in London and beyond and the Royal Canadian Mounted Police.'

Inspector Davies went on to say, 'If he met with an accident or loss of memory it is reasonable to assume that he would have been traced through routine enquiries. There is a very strong possibility that this young man was murdered and his body, so far, successfully concealed.'

Mrs Ockenden knew the logic of that but she was Kenneth's mother and she declared, 'Even though they say they believe he has been murdered, I can't give up hope. I've got to believe that he will turn up at some point. Maybe he has been in an accident,' and, as if she had discovered a new truth, 'maybe he has lost his memory or something like that and for once he hasn't been traced by routine enquiries.'

Her husband, Ken, had to apologize for thinking badly of his son. 'To be honest, I was hoping at first he'd been busted and thrown into jail somewhere, just so as I'd know he was safe.'

Another policeman, Detective Inspector Michael (Mick) Collings confided that 'the father is sort of realistic enough in saying to me he's fearing the worst – but inside he's hoping like we all are.'

The police not only checked out hospitals but by taking Kenneth's own copy of the Egon Ronay 1979 *Good Pub Guide* found amongst his belongings they checked the pubs which might have attracted him. They even banged on the doors of some infamous 'squats', houses and flats taken over by homeless dropouts and drifters, in case he had decided to abandon his normal place in society and submerge himself with the less fortunate, but there was still no trace.

Even after nine months the Ockendens had not given up hope of finding him alive. They felt it worth advertising in newspapers for information about him, even offering one thousand pounds reward for positive information. It never came. They also felt, perhaps harshly, that the police were in some way to blame for not having produced positive results. They called on their own Canadian Member of Parliament, Bill Kempling, but he could not take the matter much further.

It remained a mystery for three years and three months. Even in December 1982, to mark the third anniversary of his disappearance, police issued more photographs of Kenneth and fresh posters went up on police station notice boards throughout the capital. The Press were asked to publish yet again the appeal for assistance in finding him. Then came the cruel ironies. Stewart Goodwin, the assistant press officer at Scotland Yard, who had gone to Melrose Avenue as the liaison officer with the press after Nilsen's arrest and disclosures, had worked hard for publicity in finding the missing emigrant. Now he had to explain to reporters that Ockenden had been killed by a former Metropolitan Police probationary policeman, on the very day he disappeared. And he had met Nilsen after scanning through Egon Ronay's *Good Pub Guide* and finding the Princess Louise public house, the 'free' house noted for its jazz, jazz that Uncle Gordon had heard in that last telephone call.

From the Louise he had gone back to Melrose Avenue with Nilsen to listen to some 'rock operas' through the earphones which provided the cord to throttle him.

When Mr and Mrs Ockenden flew into London and were taken to a police station to be officially informed of the news they paused and hesitated outside. There, staring down at them, was their son's picture, framed in an appeal for information which no one had answered.

When the Ockendens were still in England, searching hospitals and mortuaries for any trace of their son, a sixteen-year-old youth was swallowed up in the vast capital. He was Martyn Brandon Duffey, a Sinclair rather than an Ockenden, a victim whom no one seemed to know was missing. No one had come to the metropolis to search for him and those who knew he had disappeared from his home town, Birkenhead, did not know where to look, or had little inclination to do so.

Martyn was born on July 6, 1963, at Clatterbridge Hospital, Bebington, a district of Birkenhead, which lies on the Wirral peninsular just across the Mersey from Liverpool. He was the son of Roy Frederick Duffey, a process worker, and Patricia Duffey, nee Brand, from 69 Goodwin Avenue, Birkenhead. The town was passed its prime then. Long before Martyn's birth it had been a watering place, a prosperous shipbuilding centre. For most of his young life it was depressed and no amount of public money seemed to improve it. When he left school at fifteen there was a shortage of jobs – and no work for him. Even though he had been to the College of Butchery and had his own set of knives with his initials 'M.B.D.' engraved on the handles.

To make matters more difficult he was torn between his parents. His mother lived at 2 Moorland Road, while his father lived on the other side of Mersey Park at 11 Seymour Street. Living there too was Martyn's older sister, by little more than a year, Hazyl Andrea Duffey. It was no easy matter for a lad of sixteen to choose between his parents or to sort out his allegiances.

When he hunted for work, which he did at first with eagerness, he gave his mother's address in Moorland Road. The Job Centre and the Department of Health and Social Security both knew it, but when he took the high road to London and did not call any more, at the offices, at his mother's address or his father's, no one seemed particularly perturbed because everybody thought he was elsewhere. No one reported him missing in Birkenhead and no one in London was any the wiser.

Only when Nilsen spoke and detectives went to that Cheshire town and traced the lad's movements and compared them with the murderer's story were they satisfied that Martyn must have been murdered between May 13 and May 19, 1980, two years and nine months before the plumber's discovery and Nilsen's confession.

A faint though still irregular pattern was emerging from the backgrounds of the victims. Ockenden may well have been the odd man out but Sinclair and

Duffey were drifting job hunters. However, detectives had to wait to solve yet another individual murder before they could find a more common denominator. This was discovered when they closed the file on William David Sutherland. Although the police had, at the time of the Sutherland enquiry, more than a suspicion that the deaths had a firm homosexual connotation, they had to rely on the details of Sutherland's record to be certain.

In his twenty-five years Billy claimed that he was a happily married man and the father of a six-year-old son. On the first count he lied, but on the second he spoke a pathetic truth.

Billy was a boy from an Edinburgh estate turned slum, a frequenter of squats and of uncertain occupation. The son of another William 'Billy' Sutherland, an ex-Royal Navy seaman and more recently a ferryman on the Stranraer–Larne route to Northern Ireland, young Billy lived on the large council housing estate at Granton in the northern part of the city of Edinburgh. Granton boasts a port and the Edinburgh gasworks; its council estate has the distinction of having as many apartments boarded up as those with glass windows intact. Local humour has it that people live behind plywood boards because they feel safer than behind glass which would in any case be due to be broken.

The truth is more sinister. The flats are boarded to prevent drifters, squatters and drug addicts from moving in. The estate where young Billy lived with his father is well known among the wastrels from the neighbouring port of Leith through which a mass of smuggled narcotics find their way to help gratify Edinburgh's growing drug problem.

It is not much of an environment in which to grow up. It never was. But it was the place Billy knew best; it was as much part of his personality as his mop of curly hair, prominent nose and infectious smile. For a time in 1977 he lived with his girl friend, Donna, in a love nest in Pennywell Gardens, Granton. Donna gave birth to Billy's child that year, a baby boy called Mark. It was no place to try to earn enough money to bring up a 'wee bairn' and when the baby was three Billy decided to seek work in London. For a time Donna and the baby stayed in London with him but then they split. He mentioned 'sending for ye both' if things worked out well but they never did and nothing more was heard of him.

Donna moved in with her parents, Mr and Mrs Kennure in nearby West Granton Loan – a Scottish word for lane – and waited. Mark's fourth, fifth and sixth birthdays went by without father. When no greetings card arrived for the lad's sixth birthday, Donna became resigned to never seeing him again.

'I could have saved him from being killed,' she said later. 'He would still be alive if I'd gone with him to London, but I did not want to leave my home, Edinburgh or Scotland. I didn't tell anyone until now, but he left me to go to London again. Now I regret it. In a way I feel it's my fault that he's dead. I should have returned there to live with him or gone and brought him back.'

She paused to recall happier days, the times when Billy worked in a London dairy and she went to the big city to see him. 'It was all right for a while but in the end I couldn't take the place any more. I came back to Auld Reekie. This time he followed me home a few months later. When we got back together later he continued to ask me to marry him and return to London, but I wouldn't I didn't like London and I just didn't want to get married, though we loved each other very much. It wasn't that I didn't love him. I just didn't

81

like London and I just didn't want to get married although he was a kind and tender lover.

'For a while I suspected that when he didn't write or come back something was wrong, even that he was dead, but even when you're told that he is definitely dead you're really still shocked with the news. I still love him and really miss him.'

When the plumber's tale was broadcast in newspapers, on radio and television in February, 1983, and the mass of human remains were discovered in the North London suburbs, Donna's mother, Mrs Elizabeth Kennure, looked at television pictures of the digging at Melrose Avenue, and knew. 'It was a terrible feeling,' she says. 'There were the police digging and me thinking "Where is our Billy?" He was there. I knew it. Don't ask me how. I just knew. It was a terrible feeling, such a strong feeling that I wanted to go to the police, then I wanted the police to contact us and tell us there and then. When we did hear officially it was still a terrible blow, as I loved Billy like a son. He was a smashing wee lad, very trusting and quiet. He had his faults; he enjoyed betting and having a drink. But he was honest and he never deserved this terrible end.'

So strongly did Billy's father feel about the loss of his son that he went back to the old Church of Scotland where he used to worship as a lad more than forty years before and asked the minister to perform 'a funeral service without a coffin'. He knew from the police the harrowing fact that the remains of his son were required, small and unidentified though they were, for forensic tests and would not merit a proper burial. Mr Sutherland and his friends dipped into their pockets to hire the best cars to take them from Granton to Leith for the service.

The eulogy from the Reverend William G. Neill on

Easter Saturday, April 2, 1983, was worthy of the famous rather than for the 'wee bit wild' son of an almost forgotten parishioner of four decades ago. 'You have come here to remember William David Sutherland and by your presence and your prayers to support one another in this time of sorrow. You remember Billy as a much loved son, as a brother, as a relative, as a friend and you bring to this service your own personal memories of someone who was very dear to you. The circumstances of Billy's death have brought to you all, and to his family in particular, a long period of silence, an agony concluded with news of the most horrible nature. You have all in the past been aware of young people who are lured away from home by the bright lights of the city and who find themselves out of their depths in the face of the worst kinds of depravity. The desperate situation of these young lives is portrayed very vividly in the tragedy of Billy and your hearts will go out to the loved ones of others who died in the same way, especially those who will never be identified.'

The Church of Scotland, with its great tradition of helping the poor and the handicapped, understood the problem only too well and the Reverend Neill acknowledged his duty to point out that whatever Billy was, and whatever he did, he was entitled to Christian forgiveness, particularly at the weekend, the Easter celebration of sacrifice. 'I did not on the other hand want to say anything platitudinous abut the boy lest something came out later at the trial that put him in a dubious light,' the minister confided after the service.

It was a wise precaution. The Church of Scotland did not know Billy, did not know of his illegitimate son, nor were they aware that whenever William David Sutherland wanted money, which was not infrequently, he, like Sinclair, went on the streets and offered his body as a male prostitute. He was known to the police as 'kamp' – Known As Male Prostitute – and to his clients by the name Doris.

Police had a difficult time when Nilsen told them he had murdered a Billy Sutherland. He remembered his name, that he was a Scot and not much more. When detectives went to the office of the Registrar of Births, Deaths and Marriages of Scotland in Princes Street, Edinburgh, the official who examined the records for them said, 'If you want a Billy or William Sutherland in his twenties and you have no further information about his place of birth, his mother's maiden name for instance, I can only tell you there are forty of them to check.'

Each Billy Sutherland record was vetted to see if that person was missing. Only when the officers came to the thirty-ninth, Billy Sutherland born in Edinburgh, registered at Leith, did they achieve any success. This Sutherland was known. And missing. A picture of him was produced and taken to Nilsen in London who said, 'That's him.'

In Christian terms young Billy was more fortunate than most of Nilsen's victims. For them there was no requiem, the practicalities of funeral services being rendered absurd for there was never a body worthy of such found at either of the suburban houses. Melrose Avenue only gave up a catalogue of bones and pens and papers. Cranley Gardens at least produced three skulls, limbs, dismembered with the boiled flesh still clinging to them. But bodies, no.

The knock on the doors of the deceased became as final as a funeral bidding. That was how it sounded in the council house at 105 Rother View Road, high on the hill on the outskirts of Rotherham, South Yorkshire.

'Is this the home of Malcolm Barlow?' asked the local constable.

'Yes,' said the woman at the door, one hand adjusting her curlers, the other putting a cigarette shakily to her mouth.

'Can I speak to Malcolm's father or mother?'

'No.'

'Why not?'

'They're both dead.'

Malcolm Barlow was born on November 28, 1957, at 66 Atlas Street, Rotherham, the ancient market town, twinned with Sheffield six miles away, its big city partner as the centre of the old steel, iron and brass industries. He was the child of Emma Barlow, nee Stanley, by her husband, Joseph Barlow, a colliery boiler fireman.

Like Stephen Sinclair, Malcolm was an epileptic. Again like Stephen the disease was hereditary. Epilepsy means seizure and it is the most important and most feared of the convulsive states. Epileptics experience loss of awareness and consciousness, suffer twitching of the muscles which they cannot control and general disturbance of the nervous system which controls all physical movements. Epilepsy is caused by an out-of-rhythm functioning of the brain cells.

When Malcolm was eleven years of age his mother died. From then on he was looked after by his sister, Doreen, the woman in curlers who answered the door to the police. She was not in the best of health herself, but she and her husband, Roy Godbar, a building worker, did their best for the orphaned boy. Schooling was difficult enough and when he had completed his education nobody was able to describe Malcolm as a prime candidate in the employment market. He had spent much of his life pining for the mother he loved, and then, while still suffering recurrent physical and mental disturbances, he went out into the world seeking work while he could not always calculate what to do next or how to do it. Small wonder that, in the words of his brother-in-law, 'he had been drifting from city to city for seven years, from the time he was seventeen to the time he vanished in September, 1981.'

Like so many jobless drifters before him London loomed large as the great panacea. One day, nobody remembers when, except that it was September 1981, Malcolm went down the bumpy steeped Rother Hill Road towards the two church spires, the two smoking chimneys and the folding hills of South Yorkshire beyond. He was never seen there again.

The next anyone heard of him was seventeen months later, by courtesy of the murderer. Nilsen had gone home to Melrose Avenue and found the lad sitting on the low wall outside his home. The boy was obviously ill. Nilsen, who had undergone a course of first aid in the Metropolitan Police, thought the boy was a junkie reacting to drugs. He did not realise the boy was having an epileptic fit. But he did call for an ambulance.

Barlow was taken to Willesden General Hospital, given advice and treatment, and then allowed to leave. Impulsively the youth went back to Melrose Avenue to say, 'Thank you. It was good of you to get me to hospital.'

'That's all right,' said Dennis. 'Come in and have a drink.' And the Good Samaritan turned out to be a strangler.

Police were able eventually to pinpoint his death as taking place on September 19, 1981, probably less than two weeks after he left Rotherham and a year and five months before Nilsen was suspected of any crime.

By the time the police passed on the news of Malcolm's death, it was being suggested in Whitehall that perhaps

Chambers and his murder squad ought to stop their enquiries. They had, with the help of Nilsen and the corroboration of evidence, last sightings, documents and other testimony, solved five murders, those of Sinclair, Ockenden, Duffey, Sutherland and Barlow. And Scotland Yard cried, 'No more.' That was enough.

The police had a mass murderer in custody, had spent more than one million pounds on policemen's overtime pay. They had sufficient evidence to satisfy the Director of Public Prosecutions in order for him to mount a legal case against Nilsen and to bring a jury to the likely conclusion that Nilsen was a mass killer. But what about the other murders? What about the relatives of the other victims? Had not Nilsen, who had so far proved to be very accurate in his bloody claims, said he had killed sixteen and then fifteen?

At the close of their investigations, Chambers and Jay had sufficient evidence to charge Nilsen with two more killings, bringing the total to seven. On instructions, however, they temporarily closed the book on May 12, 1983, three months after Nilsen's arrest, and formally charged him with killing the first five and no more. They were to add a sixth as the trial approached.

What had not gone on public record were the two fascinating cases of Graham Allan and John Howlett. Allan was another Scot, this time twenty-eight years old from 124 Carfin Road, Newarthill, on the Lanarkshire side of Glasgow. Unlike so many of Nilsen's targets, Graham was not a homosexual, nor did he give any sign that he would tolerate them let alone consort with them. He was five foot eleven inches tall, thin and wiry and exceptionally strong. When he was last in his native Scotland he playfully picked up his married sister, Linda, who at the time weighed some thirteen stone. His mother, Mrs Selina Allan, chided him, because she had recently recovered from a stroke. 'Now don't try to do that to me,' she said.

Graham, like his father, John or 'Jack' as he is known, had worked for the British Steel Corporation at the Glasgow mills. While his father had continued until he was forcibly retired, Graham tired of working there and moved to London. He did not find it easy to get work although he said he 'managed'. More important he was an adult and out of the family restraints; he could lead his own life and whatever he chose to do would be out of the ken of his somwhat stricter parents.

'Jack' Allan, for instance, a white-haired, florid faced man, did not drink. He does not celebrate even Hogmanay with anything stronger than a cup of tea. Neither he nor his wife approved of couples setting up home outside marriage, and they were 'put out' when they learned that Graham had fallen in love with Lesley Mead, mother of a ten-year-old child. Mrs Allan, a comfortably built homely woman, did not like it at all.

'I told her, "Why don't you go to the civic office here and have a quiet wedding? We will give you the money to furnish your own place." But Lesley is a Londoner. She wasn't interested. She wanted to stay down south. In my mind she wasn't the right girl for Graham. She was some years older, and she already had a child. I thought she had some sort of hold over Graham, but then a mother can't pick a son's wife for him, can she?'

Graham brought Lesley home to Newarthill during April, 1982. They returned to London together, then Graham came up on his own for a while during August and then went back. 'When we didn't hear from him we began to get worried, particularly at Christmas time. We didn't even get a Christmas card and that was very unusual. We thought there was something wrong so we wrote, but didn't get any answer to our letters.'

The Allans used to write to their son at 30 Shorrolds Road in Fulham, but Hammersmith and Fulham Council, which acquired the property several years before, denied they had had any tenants by the name of Allan or Mead living there. Mrs Allan thought the couple were about to move, but there had never been a forwarding address. 'It was as if they had both vanished from the face of the earth.'

The truth was more brutal. Graham had first come from Glasgow to London when he was sixteen and he had fairly quickly been engulfed by the sick and sleazy sector of London life, so much so that he became a registered drug addict. In medical terms that gave him a certain status, a certain right to drugs, but he craved more and more.

He had known Lesley Mead for some years, since she had been the barmaid at a public house near Leicester Square. Lesley had three children, all in the care of the local council, and was quite willing to look after Graham. But it was an up and down relationship, in which both showed their hot tempers. In such quarrels Graham, the petty thief, extremely strong and abnormally violent when in drink, would win.

Then he would go missing, usually on a thieving expedition to finance his drug addiction. This time, however, he did not return. 'When he did not come back I was terribly upset. Usually he only stormed off for a couple of days. I just had to assume that he had taken an overdose and died quietly somewhere.'

By the time Lesley told this to the police they had matched one of the three skulls found at Cranley Gardens with an X-ray plate showing a fractured jaw which Graham had sustained in an accident some years previously. It was a simple matter for the dental surgeon who had Graham's records to say the skull belonged to him.

As a result, on August 1, 1983, almost six months after the first remains were found at Cranley Gardens and Melrose Avenue, and just five days before Graham's twenty-ninth birthday, the police called at his Scottish home. Mother was busying herself as usual in the kitchen, the pride of a well-kept, clean, tidy and bright home. Jack was tending the roses in the small but perfectly cultivated corner patch of the back yard. Even the hardened police officers, who had brought tragic news to so many, had to admit, 'It was very hard for them to take.'

As for Howlett, just a week before the trial, police charged Nilsen with his murder. It had been a long and hard task tracing the victim. All Nilsen could remember was that one of his wretched prey was 'John the Guardsman from High Wycombe.' One detective was sent to verify all the Brigade records at the depots of the Scots, Welsh, Irish, Coldstream and Grenadier Guards, but there was not one missing John there. Nor was there a missing John on the books of High Wycombe police.

Working on the theory that the victim frequented the West End of London and was someone who had been in trouble, police checked again the records of the people who lived in High Wycombe but had been interviewed or prosecuted by police at West End Central police station, Savile Row. This research revealed the identity of John Peter Howlett of High Wycombe, who used to be in fairly regular trouble with the police but had then 'gone straight' or missing. Further enquiries showed that Howlett had never been near the door of an Army recruiting office let alone a Guards depot, and a few questions in the right Soho pubs yielded the information that he liked to pass himself off as an ex-Guardsman, a well-known ploy to ingratiate himself with homosexuals and then rob them.

When police took Howlett's picture from the Criminal Records Office file and showed it to Nilsen the murderer's face lit up again.

'That's him. That's John the Guardsman,' he exclaimed.

Howlett was the older son of Peter Frederick Howlett, an electrical inspector, and his wife Margaret Joan, of Cambridge Crescent, High Wycombe.

John turned up in his home town only once or twice a year, Michael, his younger brother, was able to tell the police. When the fairground cavalcade of mobile homes, steam engines, dodgems, roundabouts and coconut shies rumbled through High Wycombe John would join them. The travelling folk would make their pitch for a week here, ten days there. John might work one night, two or even five, depending on how his fancy took him. As the cash built up in his pocket John knew when he had had enough – of money or work. The fairground people paid daily so once he had sufficient he would walk out of the show ground and head for London.

'He knew where to spend his money and how to spend it quickly,' said Michael.

Which was where Nilsen met so many of his intended victims, in West End public houses like the Salisbury in St Martin's Lane, and the Golden Lion in Dean Street, Soho.

Seven

The Golden Lion in Dean Street in the heart of the
sleazy square mile of Sly City, otherwise known as
Soho, is not the sort of pub in which to meet a maiden
aunt before taking her to the theatre. Any one of the
good restaurants in the neighbourhood, or the archi-
tectural subtleties of the bombed remains of St Anne's,
the prostitutes' church, opposite, would be better
venues to distract her attention from the mass of sex
shops, strip shows and hard core porn movies showing
in cluttered premises scattered through the maze of
streets. And from the Golden Lion.

Attractive enough from the outside, the four-storey
public house, with its mock Tudor facade, more recent
oak beam rendering and leaded lights, is really the not-
so-happy hunting ground for male homosexuals. Far
from being in any way Golden, the Lion is dominated
by dull red carpeting and plastic seating round the
walls.

A stranger entering through the corner door where
Dean Street joins Romilly Street might well get a
surprise, and a woman could be excused for making a
rapid exit. Almost every pair of eyes would tell her
that she is not welcome. For they belong to gays of all
shapes, sizes, colours, young and muscle bound, biceps
rippling under lurid tattoos, well-dressed businessmen
trying not to look ashamed and embarrassed at being
spotted there, the old and seedy past their time, but
still with their sexual fantasies. Racial and class barriers

are non-existent, yet other stronger ones are erected against outsiders.

Strangers will be served quickly and efficiently but unless they are obviously 'cruising' – the jargon for seeking homosexual company – they will be ignored by the clan. One clue to those who are not obviously gay is whether they pick up a copy of *Capital Gay*, the epicene newspaper, always on the bar for anyone to read. Most customers stand drinking alone, their eyes flitting from person to person, weighing them up, assessing their chances of success, company, conversation, sex or all three, wondering whether it will cost them money and how much.

Very few mince their walk. Not all lisp their words. Occasionally a 'darling' is thrown into the conversation, or an effeminate gay, when addressed by a masculine name will say, 'Why Jack! That's a boy's name, isn't it?' But then there will always be the habitues who pat their hair into place, pout their lips, blow kisses, dab their make-up or indulge in the thousand and one affectations traditionally given to women and older or theatrical women at that.

The majority conduct normal conversations about current affairs, politics, weather, or God. For the Gay Christian Movement has recruited customers to go to St Botolph's Church in the City of London to listen to sermons about Christian relationships and ethical potential and non-Christian sexism. They sing 'Now thank we all our God . . . for all the things he's done' meaning, to them, for showing them the richness and diversity of human sexuality. They have even sung their own hymn:

> We come with self inflicted pains
> Of broken trust and chosen wrong,
> Half free, half bound by inner chains,

By social forces swept along,
By powers and systems close confined,
Yet seeking hope for human kind.

They are indeed a diverse people. The law has freed them from the Victorian concepts of homosexuality, that their sexual acts are an abomination (as the Bible says) and that they should suffer anything up to life imprisonment for homosexual acts. After the Wolfenden Report of 1957 and the change of the law a decade later they became free to practise their homosexuality in private providing they were consenting adults. This was to protect minors – in this case those under the age of eighteen – from being corrupted.

What that has meant is that homosexuals who find satisfaction with fellow deviates tend not to display their affections in public in the hope of being accepted by their fellow creatures. Those who cannot achieve that gratification tend to gravitate to those places, and particularly public houses, which attract the like minded. Places like the Golden Lion.

Nilsen, the loner, would stand at the bar of the Lion looking for someone to share his company, to talk and drink. Hs appearance was not in the least gay. He was more soberly and smartly dressed than most around him. He preferred not to look towards the Royal Box, that part of the bar said to be the preserve of Queens. Nilsen declared that he did not like them. He had had to make use of their company when he was desperate for physical friendship. He preferred, he insisted, less commercially minded companions.

Besides, like many practising homosexuals he feared the phoneys, those who offered themselves but then beat up and robbed their newly found acquaintances. 'Rolling', as it was known, is a hazard among those of his ilk.

'Large handbag, darling?' someone would shout from behind the bar and Nilsen would pay for a pint of lager, for such it was called in that company. He would sip it, look around the bar again over the rim of the glass. And that is how he first saw Douglas Stewart, a shock-haired Scot with a soft Highland accent.

Stewart frequented the pub on his nights off, attracted, he claims, not by the gay fraternity, but by the number of his fellow Scots who used the bar. Life for Stewart, twenty-five years old that November 1980, was not much fun. Like thousands of others he had become frustrated with the lack of opportunities north of the border. Even after two years training as a chef at the Gleneagles Hotel, the five star establishment at Auchterarder, Perthshire, he was unable to get a worthwhile job in Scotland. Like many other Scots before him he took the high road to London where he secured a temporary junior kitchen job at the no star twenty-bed Holland Park Hotel in Ladbroke Terrace, the racially mixed Bohemian area of west London. He complained that the work was hard, the conditions indifferent, the pay low and the hours split.

His day started at 6 a.m. in time for breakfast. The moment that meal was completed the preparations for lunch began. Afternoons he could snatch a few hours' sleep before preparing dinner. It was a good day, he claimed, if he could get out of the kitchen by 9 p.m. and call the rest of the day his own.

The long, hot gruelling routine was made a little more tolerable by the presence of his girl friend, Dawn, from the Elephant and Castle, who worked as a chamber maid at the same hotel. But there was still nothing he liked better than to finish work and go to Soho and take a drink with the people he knew best, the Scots. That was his plan when in the week beginning November 9, 1980, he was off duty earlier than usual with a day off on the morrow, a welcome respite from the never ending toil at the Holland.

That night all eyes switched to his as he walked into the bar, his curly hair catching the light as it bobbed in time to his gentle walk. Some of the faces in the Golden Lion he knew, many he did not. Nilsen he recognized from the other end of the bar from previous visits. It was a face he had seen often, drinking with different groups of people, talking a lot. They had never met before, never spoken, but as new company arrived, old company left, they found themselves in the same group. Nilsen introduced himself as 'Desi'.

It did not take long for them to discover their common interests. Both were Scotsmen. Both had been trained as chefs. Within a short time they had also had their differences, a brief argument whether *à chasseur* and *à forestiere* are both styles of-cooking, the huntsman's and the forester's, or whether one is a sauce and the other a manner of presentation. It did not damage the exchange and for most of the time Stewart was content to listen while Nilsen talked.

Stewart would not describe himself as clever, but is overwhelmingly confident of his own ability to survive. He has an instinctive street wisdom like many of his fellow Scots which makes him satisfied to let others lead the talk, make the suggestions, leaving him to be on guard against being put upon or cheated. It was no burden for him to remain silent while the slightly supercilious and wordy Nilsen held the pub floor, and he only joined the conversation when he was expected to do so.

They were an interesting pair since both were Highland Scots, Stewart who had retained his accent from Wick in the far north and Nilsen, from Fraserburgh in the north east, who had, in middle class affectation, abandoned his. What they probably did not know about each other was that they could both be articulate and rational one minute and the next very short-tempered if something, even for no apparent reason, upset them.

They both drank a lot that evening, Stewart more than he had paid for, by some token a good measure of the success of the evening, and while his newly found friend, Dennis, did not mind paying slightly more than his guest he had at least gained a companion. He even suggested that the whole group should return to his flat for a drink.

'You'll come back with us to my place,' said Nilsen as if it was a foregone conclusion. 'What sort of spirits do you drink?'

'Vodka,' said Stewart quickly and watched Nilsen's back as the host ordered a bottle of vodka and cans of lager to take with them.

Outside on the pavement, the conversation continued, some suggesting they went for a Chinese meal, some to see a strip show, until Stewart found himself alone with Nilsen. Only the two of them were returning to Dennis's place. What did that matter? He suspected that Nilsen was a homosexual but if he wanted to buy the drinks and entertain him that was his decision. If there was any trouble Stewart was confident that he could defend himself if not with his sharp tongue then at least with his fists. The only thing that bothered him was that since Nilsen had jawed Scotland to death, and exhausted the recipe books, what other subjects could he expect?

Nilsen was talking about the civil service and his interest in trade union affairs as they entered the taxi and Nilsen gave the address. 'Take us to Melrose Avenue.' By which time Stewart was, as he put it, 'a wee bit fu',' so much so that he did not gather exactly where his host lived and was unaware of the finer points Nilsen wanted to make about Whitehall and organized labour. He remembered only getting out of the cab and later remembering that 195 Melrose Avenue was dimly lit and that he stumbled slightly as they made their way to a ground floor flat at the rear. Considering Nilsen's generosity in buying a bottle of vodka, and a take-away pack of lager, and paying for the taxi ride over a good five-mile journey it seemed strange that he had brought him back to such a poorly furnished flat, the furniture of which consisted of little more than a couple of armchairs, a television set and a two-tier bunk bed. Still it was out of the November night air and Nilsen quickly poured a lager and handed it to him.

'Do you want some vodka?'

'I'm all right just now.'

'Well, you might as well know I've got it here.'

'Okay then.'

Stewart had the taste for alcohol, but he slightly blanched when he saw Nilsen take a ten ounce glass and fill it almost to the brim with the colourless liquid. Stewart had been a part-time barman and knew that he was being offered half a pint of spirit with no room for any tonic, orange or other additives. It was too much.

'I really don't want that much,' he said.

'Go on. Drink it,' said Nilsen, an offended tone creeping into his voice.

The visitor took a sip of the vodka so as not to appear ungrateful, but put it down by the side of the armchair and returned to his lager.

Nilsen had turned on the television for Stewart to watch but had chosen to don earphones to listen to records from his music master.

Suddenly Stewart realized he must have fallen asleep. He woke with a start, noticed the television was blank and looking at his watch saw it was after one o'clock in the morning. 'Is that the time?' he asked sleepily. 'I really ought to be getting back.'

'You might as well stay, get the first tube in the morning.'

Stewart pondered the invitation. The first underground train service would not be until five or six o'clock. But then it was growing cold outside, and there was nothing he actually disliked about his host. Talked a bit too much. Poured daft drinks in large quantities. But what the hell? He seemed all right.

'Have one of the bunks?' said Nilsen, indicating that the stereo equipment on them could easily be moved.

'I'll be okay in the chair, thanks,' said Stewart, loosening his tie and covering himself with his coat.

Nilsen took off his jeans, shirt and socks and pulled himself up to the top of the two bunks. 'Will you have some more vodka?' he asked as he settled down.

'No thanks.'

'Why don't you come up here with me?' The homosexual invitation did not surprise Stewart. He had been half expecting it and his answer was ready.

'No, I don't do things like that.'

'Fair enough,' said Nilsen, turning his back on his guest, presumably not wanting to show he was peeved. Stewart closed his eyes, listened carefully for the slightest sound that might signal another approach, this time a physical one, but it never came. Within a few minutes the armchair visitor had turned on one side, his legs and knees together, and slept.

He had no idea of the time when he awoke. He was only conscious of aching and being stiff from trying to sleep in the confines of an armchair. He wanted to stretch but found he could not. Heady, puzzled, his senses clouded by vodka it took him a few seconds to realize that his ankles had been tied to the legs of the chair. Then he felt something at his neck. His loosened tie was being carefully moved from under his collar to encircle his bare throat.

In a second Stewart was fully awake. His tie was crossed right over his windpipe and the young Scot knew that he was in danger. The tie was closing round his neck, tighter and tighter. He was being throttled. He was literally seeing red and knew that within seconds he would black out. He could see Nilsen in front of him for the lights had not been switched out. There was no hatred or badness in his eyes. Nor was there any hint that the attack was going to stop.

'Another second or two and I would have been gone,' recalls Stewart. 'He was putting his knee on my chest. All I was thinking was how to get him off before I was a goner. All this time his expression didn't change. It was uncanny. Despite what he was doing he looked perfectly normal.'

There were few options open to Stewart. He could not kick out because his feet were tied. He could not aim a proper punch because of the restriction of the chair and Nilsen's knee on his chest, but because Nilsen's face was now close to his Stewart tried to claw his eyes. He missed but caught him on the cheek bone, scratching his face and drawing blood. The superficial wound probably saved Stewart's life. For Nilsen pulled back the moment he was scratched but not far enough to avoid a blow from Stewart springing from the chair, though his feet were still tied, knocking his murderous host to the floor.

Breathing heavily, Stewart snatched up his tie and quickly went to free his ankles. Nilsen was still lying on the floor and Stewart fell on top of him, putting his knees on his opponent's arms, pressing into Nilsen's biceps and threatening to smash Nilsen's pretty face.

'Take my money. Take my money,' screamed Nilsen.

'I don't want your money. I have money of my own. You tried to kill me, you bastard.'

'I never touched you,' protested Nilsen.

'Try it again now.'

The tone of Nilsen's voice changed and he spoke very quietly in a way that Stewart says he will never forget. 'I could kill you now.'

Stewart's recollection is that 'it seems ludicrous now, since I was on top of him. He was under my weight, but his words, "I could kill you now" took all the anger out of the situation. It stopped me dead in my tracks.'

For a while Stewart did not move from his position of physical domination. He stayed where he was on top of his attacker and accused him a second time of trying to kill. Again Nilsen denied it.

'I never touched you. It's all in your mind, your imagination.'

'I'll still go to the police.'

'The police? They'll never believe you. They're bound to take my word for it. Like I told you in the pub, I'm a respectable civil servant.'

Stewart thought about what Nilsen had said, eased the pressure on him and stood up. It was time to go. He turned his back to Nilsen and reached for his coat, sensing rather than seeing Nilsen getting up from the floor. When he looked round Nilsen had moved very quickly and was standing on the other side of the room, an eighteen-inch saw-edged knife in his hand. Nilsen looked somewhat theatrically at the blade. Then at Stewart. He was clearly deciding on whether or not to use it. Stewart looked at his attacker and decided he was not prepared to take the risk.

'Put it down. Put it down and don't be silly.'

'I didn't attack you.'

'No. I suppose I must have been dreaming. I'm all

right now. Come into the kitchen. Let me wash the blood off your face. I'm sorry.'

Nilsen responded to Stewart's sudden change of mood. It was the clever thing to do. He walked into the kitchen, put the knife away in a drawer. Yet Nilsen's outward appearance, his attitude, speech except for that one fearful line, 'I could kill you now,' had remained the same as it had been in the Golden Lion all those hours ago.

Stewart could not understand it, certainly not the next question.

'Have another drink?' Nilsen asked.

Stewart wanted to be rid of Nilsen, but as the immediate danger was gone the best way to preserve the peaceful mood was to pretend to agree with his peculiar host. So he accepted the offer, took the lager and sat gulping it from the can, trying to appear as if there was no hurry. At last Stewart said, 'I'll go and wait for the tube,' and left.

His watch still gave the time as only 3.30 a.m., so he would have to wait at least another two hours for a train, but he stepped out of the house into the cold night air, walked the length of two or three houses and then broke into a run. At the first telephone box he glanced behind him to see if he was being followed, went inside and dialled 999 for the police. Nor did he have to wait long before a Panda car pulled up alongside.

'What's going on here, then?' asked the constable.

'This fellow tried to murder me. Look!' Stewart showed the policeman the red marks round his neck. The police nodded, caught the smell of beer on his breath, and invited him to get into their car.

'We'd better go round there then,' said the other officer. 'What's the address?'

'One nine five Melrose Avenue. His name's Nilsen. Calls himself Dennis.'

The two policemen looked knowingly at each other. One of the constables strode up to the door leaving Stewart with his colleague by the car. It took some time for the officer at the door to get an answer but Nilsen emerged giving the impression that he had just risen from his normal slumbers.

As Stewart was to recall later, 'Nilsen denied everything I had told the police. He gave them the impression that we were going out together and it was just a lovers' quarrel in a homosexual romance. That made me mad. It struck me then that that was what he meant when he said earlier that the police would never believe me. I told the police that I had left my tie. It was still there and that would prove it. It was brown with diagonal stripes. They both went inside, leaving me on the pavement, but there was no tie there, they said. He must have hidden it.'

When the police came out of the house they asked Stewart where he could be contacted. He gave them the address of his brother in Northwood, Middlesex, sixteen miles from London where he planned to spend the rest of his break from work. After that there was no contact, and there remains a disagreement of great importance between the Metropolitan Police and Douglas Stewart. Stewart maintains that from the first moment the word 'homosexual' is mentioned, the police tend to show very little interest. 'I never heard from the police again. I thought about contacting them, but once back at the kitchen of the Holland Park Hotel I was so busy I did nothing more about it. They were not interested.

'Remember this, I told the police that he had attacked me. I showed them the marks round my throat where the tie cut into me. I talked to them about the knife. I wanted them to charge him with attempted murder there and then, but they did not. If they had done so, then possibly several people who are now dead would be alive. The police made a bad mistake. They let him off when he attacked me. Now we don't know how many more he killed at Melrose Avenue after he took me back there. Or Cranley Gardens after that.'

The Metropolitan Police version is this. Stewart could not be contacted at his brother's address. He did not at any time give the address of the Holland Park Hotel. When the police could not contact Stewart they thought he would contact them. When he did not do so they assumed that he wished to drop the complaint. Bearing in mind that he was smelling of drink when he called the police, that it was from a call box in a district which was strange to him, that it was 3.30 in the morning and there was a homosexual connotation, the police did not feel it would be in the public interest to pursue the complaint. They also felt that he did not appear to be seriously injured.

There the matter rested for two years and four months. That was in February, 1983, when the search of Melrose Avenue produced what police dramatically referred to as a 'death list'. Chambers and Jay thought that Douglas Stewart, named on the list, might be dead and his bones broken and charred under the mounds of funeral pyres. They called his brother in Northwood, who referred them to his mother in Milton Keynes, who directed them to a caravan in Thurso, the most northerly town in the Scottish mainland, nearly seven hundred miles from the scene of the crime.

At last they found and made contact with Douglas Stewart.

This time they did take his complaint seriously, whether or not he had been drinking, whether or not he had had a homosexual relationship with Nilsen. He was warned that he might be required as a witness in the case of Regina versus Nilsen.

Police thought he would be believed, so they charged Nilsen that he did attempt to murder Douglas Stewart at Melrose Avenue between November 9 and November 12, 1980.

Eight

Police rarely charge anyone with an offence in the middle of the night. With Stewart's breath smelling strongly of alcohol they were unlikely to take any further action beyond the doorstep enquiries at 195 Melrose Avenue. Both constables knew that in the harsh sobriety of the morning that inevitably follows the indulgences of the night before people like Stewart are apt to say, 'You know, that was really my fault last night. We'd both had a few to drink.' And there the matter would end.

Nilsen's explanation was perfectly plausible, and, according to the police, Stewart was not to be found at the address he had given them. Police claimed that they made three different calls to his brother's home at Northwood, Middlesex, and as he was not there it was added reason to assume that he did not want to proceed with his complaint.

Police insist that they even left a note for Stewart, but Stewart's brother says that he was at home with his wife throughout that period and no policemen called. Stewart says he received no note.

Many contemporary criticisms of the police are not merely politically motivated but come from fringe groups with extreme ideas on how to run the police without Parliamentary or local authority control. Many are patently unjust, but someone in authority must ask in the Nilsen case: why could a mass murderer commit such a gory succession of crimes over a period of almost three years and then only be discovered by accident when a plumber, summoned by a handful of people who could not flush their lavatories, found human remains in a blocked drain? True, so many victims were not reported missing but should the police have acted sooner? On Stewart's testimony the answer must surely be, 'Yes.'

Even though Nilsen was a respectable civil servant, and a former probationary policeman, it seems frightening that his word should have been accepted so quickly and finally against that of the complainant.

What is to be made of the word of microbiology honours graduate Robert Wilson, Bachelor of Science, University College, London? When the Nilsen case began to dominate the news in February, 1983, he had just begun studying for his master's degree. One morning he spent some time reading the *Daily Mirror* account of the plumber's find at 23 Cranley Gardens. The time he spent with his paper irritated his mother who suggested that it was time he went to his lectures. But murder fascinated twenty-six-year-old Wilson, who had consumed the biography of Sir Bernard Spilsbury, the pathologist who dominated the forensic science field for so long, and who worked from University College, London, where Wilson studied. Wilson also had considerable knowledge of other mass murderers, like Heath, Haig and Christie, so it was hardly surprising that he was riveted by the unfolding story.

When he returned home that evening he stared at the television screen showing the picture of 195 Melrose Avenue, the lone sentinel policeman on the gate, the snow falling freely around him: 'Mum!' he called to the kitchen, 'do you remember the night . . .?'

The night of August 23, 1981, seventeen months before, Wilson had walked his dog from their council house in Dollis Hill Lane through Gladstone Park towards Melrose Avenue which emerges opposite the park entrance. As he returned in the lane at about 10.30 p.m. he saw on the pavement by one of the street lamps a supermarket carrier bag that appeared to have fallen out of the waste paper bin, split open as it hit the flagstones. His dog, a black and white terrier, Tim, was interested, too.

'I saw a load of meat-type stuff, flesh glinting in the light,' he remembers. 'So I prodded at it with a stick. I couldn't see exactly what it was so I went home to get a torch so I could check properly. There was no mistaking what I saw: a heart, lungs, windpipe and larynx, all attached together. It was all wet and covered in blood.

'With my qualifications and interests I obviously knew some anatomy and have seen human organs before, in hospitals, museums and laboratories. But as I am not an anatomist I would not swear as a scientist that they were human. It would take an expert to identify precisely what they were.'

Wilson went to the nearest kiosk two hundred yards away, called the police, was answered by Willesden Green station and transferred to Kilburn.

'I'm enquiring to find out if there's been a murder committed anywhere,' he began voicing his suspicions.

'Why's that?' said the police voice.

'Because I've found a heart, lungs, windpipe and larynx, all attached together in a plastic bag.'

'They are from animals, aren't they?' the suspicious tone of authority asked.

'I'm not at all sure that they are,' said Wilson, wondering.

'We'll send someone round,' the officer said suddenly.

Wilson went back to the lamp-post, noticed now that there were three bags in all, and waited for the police to arrive. They came, he remembers, in two police cars, not one. One of the constables spoke with a Welsh accent. They asked him again what had happened and he repeated the story. When he prodded the bag with his stick they told him to leave it alone. Neither of the officers was keen to touch the contents of the bags, and as far as Wilson could gauge neither knew very much about anatomy.

'Is that a lung or something?' said one.

'No, it's the heart.'

'Is that the backbone?'

'No, that's the windpipe.'

The policemen were clearly uncertain what to do, but they did realize that it was a health hazard and said so. They took Wilson's name and address, said they would take care of it and sent him home. When he walked by next morning there were no bags, only the barest of bloodstains reminding him of his find of the previous night. He assumed they had taken them away. He thought he might hear from them again but never did. Wilson gave the matter little more attention until he was seated in front of the television that cold February evening of 1983 and reminded his mother what had happened.

Wilson worried about it that night, slept poorly, and next day called the *Daily Mirror* and spoke to reporter Douglas Bence. Bence advised Wilson to go to the police, and remind them of the incident, for it may well help detectives in what the telecaster was describing as 'the biggest murder investigation of the century.'

As a result, police tried to find the entries in the books which would have logged Wilson's original telephone call, registered the answer of the police cars and the report of one or both of the constables who attended the strange find at the lamp post. No such incident had been reported in writing. For that the police offered three reasons: either the call was not logged so the police officers, satisfied, took no action because none was necessary; the matter was entered but the records had been lost in the transfer of papers from one police station to another during repairs; or the incident, so graphically described, did not occur.

The issue has become a stalemate. Police have been unable to answer the question satisfactorily. They certainly have not been able to discredit the story of the graduate microbiologist. And they are faced with the fact that the generally reliable Dennis Nilsen told them that in August, 1981, he was disposing of some of his victims, whose remains, we know, were dissected, left lying about the flat, put under floorboards, taken up, burned and sometimes disposed of on waste ground. Like Gladstone Park? Or in a receptacle provided on lamp posts for the tidy of the district?

Nor was that all. Two other incidents which the police dismissed at the time were to emerge and demand answers as the Nilsen case progressed. After he had killed for the first time and before he was eventually arrested at least two other people complained that Nilsen had tried to murder them by strangulation. One was a Japanese gentleman, Toshimitsu Ozawa, from Fukishima, the Japanese prefecture of north Honshu.

Early one morning he rushed into a police station and assaulted the officer at the front desk with such a flurry of heavily accented words that the officer failed to separate or understand any two of them.

'What's the matter now?' the desk man placated him. 'Calm down and maybe we can get to the bottom of this.'

Many aspects of police work are mundane and frustrating. The paper work is non productive. The 'street wisdom' of the petty crook who knows and thinks more about his rights under the law than of keeping the peace is thwarting. The arrogance of the hardened criminal with money who hides behind lawyers and the small print of police procedure is a pain. Often it is foreigners, welcome to seek sanctuary in Britain without necessarily understanding the language or the customs or the law, who neutralize the police operations. They need time spent on them to tell them what is wrong under our criminal laws, how to redress the wrong and what the result might be.

'What's the matter now? Calm down and maybe we can get to the bottom of this.'

The Japanese cooled for a moment.

'Now let's start at the beginning. Your name, first, please, sir, then your address,' said the sergeant lifting his ball point pen and hoping that his words had not sounded too patronizing. He looked up expectantly at the chef from the Orient: he really could have come from anywhere there, Singapore, China, Hong Kong, Malaya, Indonesia, for there were, to the policeman's eyes, another thousand million who looked the same. The policeman did not get the information he wanted. The man from the East was throwing words again.

He had met this stranger in a pub on his night off, gone back to the stranger's apartment in Cranley Gardens for another drink. Three times the man advanced towards him, holding a tie. This time there was a struggle. He waved all eight fingers desperately at the marks on his neck and pulled away the grey T-shirt that had once been white for the officer to see for himself. The policeman looked sympathetically at the angry red marks, still unable to write anything down.

'You go round, sir, go round to this man Desi,' the Japanese insisted. 'You go round and arrest this man. Put him in jail. This man is dangerous. You British justice,' and he prodded the air towards the officer with his forefinger. 'You British justice. You do something.'

The officer could only produce his greatest weapon, patience. He was not going to worry how he told it but only that he was understood. Things were not, 'like it is where you come from, maybe,' but a statement would have to be made, carrying the complainant's name, address, occupation, and then having made the complaint he would have to sign it that it was true. If, as a result, anyone was prosecuted in the courts of law he would be expected to attend, take the oath to swear to tell the truth, the whole truth and nothing but the truth. Then, and only then, if everybody agreed that what he had said about this man, Desi, was true, then he would no doubt be punished. Was that not what he wanted?

The injured party listened carefully, grunted occasionally and uttered the odd word that did not sound particularly polite. So far as he was concerned that may be British justice but it was not on his terms. He was a busy man, a chef, he might have to take time off work, he might lose his work permit if he dared to appear in a British court. People might think he was the guilty party. All of which was followed by another hysterical outburst, with a few more inexplicable phrases, and the murder victim who might have been, vanished as fast as he had appeared.

Back to the canteen tea, now cold in the mug, the officer shrugged. If there was no complaint there could be no action. But Nilsen again confirmed a story. He had met Toshimitsu Ozawa, a chef, in the Green Man public house, actually on Muswell Hill, on New Year's Eve, 1982, and had taken him home to Cranley Gardens and tried to kill him. That was only forty days before Nilsen's arrest, but by the time Murder Squad detectives went on the trail of Ozawa he had vanished, possibly back to mountainous Fukushima.

Police were content to play down the matter as a typical complaint by a not untypical foreigner who did not understand or did not want to comply with the elementary rule that a complainant must be prepared to support his clamour.

Then Nilsen remembered another one that 'got away,' the Chinese cook, Andrew Ho, who had stepped out of a Chinese restaurant in the heart of Soho after a row with the manager.

Mr Ho had not exactly complained to the police that Nilsen had attempted to murder him. His chief worry was that he might have murdered Nilsen.

The pattern was now as familiar to the police as the Chinese willow is to the Orientals. He met Nilsen in a public house, went back to his home, then in Melrose Avenue, for a drink and had fallen asleep in a chair. He, too, had awoken with a shock to find he was being strangled.

Apologetically, the visitor explained that he was not highly skilled in the martial arts and he was a small man, trapped in an armchair, barely able to move. But he had suddenly reached out for a brass candlestick nearby and smashed it down with all his might on Nilsen's head. He could not explain how he had done it. His speed, aim and delivery had astonished him, but Nilsen had folded up and crashed down lifeless to the floor. The Chinese rubbed his neck again for comfort and to draw the police attention to the burning of the skin from the strangulation.

Anxious not to awaken the rest of the household he had tiptoed from the scene and gone home. Then, next morning, stricken with fear that he might have killed in self defence he had decided to go to a police station and explain. Would they please go to see the man in

Melrose Avenue who might still be unconscious, even dead?

A telephone call, a despatched Panda car, a doorstep interview by two policemen and police were satisfied that Nilsen was alive, had suffered no permanent damage, just had a hangover, he said, more than one too many the night before. No, he did not remember any Chinese but then he had invited a few people from a public house for a drink, had had too much himself, fell on the floor cracking his head, and that was that.

Meanwhile, back at Kensington police station, for that was the nearest the Chinese could find, he was told the result of the inquiries, and he was told that if he wished to make a complaint he would have to give his name, address and occupation, sign a statement, go to court, et cetera. No, the Chinese chef did not think so. He was glad no permanent damage had been done. When the police went to look for the Chinese he was still alive and living in Switzerland and did not want to return to press his complaint.

By then, the Murder Squad were collecting a file on the ones 'that got away.' In addition to Stewart, the Japanese and the Chinese there were at least five others, said Nilsen, one even a juvenile. If the police had heard of them on very different dates, years apart, at widely separated police stations they could not be expected to have collated the complaints. Or could they? They learned about them, the second time round and too late, from Nilsen himself. He remembered the Chinese, as he remembered other intended victims with the help of a diary, documents and other possessions found at both Melrose Avenue and Cranley Gardens. He had picked up Ho on Halloween, October 31, 1979, three years and three months before he was arrested.

But, asked Nilsen, did they know about yet another,

a blond homosexual who was actually known as 'Blondie'? He did not know much more about him, but if they would take the trouble to find him, 'Blondie' would be able to help them about another incident that happened at Cranley Gardens in May, 1982. Scotland Yard appealed for help, issued a photofit picture, and into a much-sought limelight stepped Khara Le Fox.

'It's a name, darling, I took when I was in a summer show as a dancer. Do you like it?'

His story was simple enough to those who knew the Nilsen file but it had a remarkable twist. He had gone to the Black Cap public house in Camden High Street, north-west London, because he was staying in a nearby hostel. He had had to quit his dancing troupe in Blackpool after a fight with another gay which had resulted in him being struck in the mouth causing an unsightly scar.

As lonely at that moment as Nilsen, he recalled, 'You know how you can feel someone's eyes on you? Well, his eyes were on me.'

Nilsen joined him, told him that he had been a policeman, now worked for social services not far away at Kentish Town Road. Probably because he realized that Le Fox was a more practised homosexual than many of his pick-ups he did not offer to help the hostel dweller find a job. He did, however, invite him back home to Cranley Gardens.

Nilsen, the over-generous host, poured large measures of whisky for the dancer and in the early hours of the morning offered the visitor a sleeping bag, which, he warned, had a 'dangerous' zip fastener. He used the word 'dangerous' and was accurate, for a few hours later Le Fox awoke to find the zip fastener tightening around his neck with Nilsen pulling the tightening tag.

115

Le Fox could only recall, 'I remember saying, "what are you doing?" or something like that, but I passed out. When I came round I was in a bath of cold water looking up at this Desi and saying, "What are you doing?" He just stared at me then put his hands on my shoulders and pushed me under. I could do nothing to stop him and while my head was underneath I saw him staring at me. I still can. I thought to myself, "so this is what death feels like." '

'I passed out and woke up on the lounge settee with his dog, Bleep, licking my face.'

Some of that night was a mental fog to Le Fox. He could remember that 'I became sensible and said to Nilsen, "Did you try to kill me last night?" He said, "No, You nearly choked in that sleeping bag and I saved you." '

Then, according to Le Fox, he asked Nilsen, 'Why was I in a bath of cold water and you tried to push me under?'

Nilsen (he said) replied, 'You were in shock after choking in the bag and that is the best way to treat it.'

Murder Squad detectives listened to the gay dancer in amazement. His story was scarcely believable. Yet he insisted that he decided to make light of the matter and even went for a walk in the woods with Nilsen before going to see friends in the East End. Suddenly he felt a blow on the back of the head and hit hard ground. 'I was stunned but he roughly jerked me to my feet with a fixed stare. Perhaps that was another lucky escape . . .'

Would a jury believe Le Fox? He was an admitted homosexual, he was promiscuous, he was thinking of having a sex change operation, but his story had more than the smell of truth. Nilsen's method of operation, the public-house pick-up, the attempted strangulation followed a pattern now well known to the police, even

116

though the sleeping bag method of strangulation was new to them, as was the attempted drowning.

'I realize how lucky I am to be alive,' said Le Fox. 'I still have nightmares about the whole thing. Of course my way of life puts me in some risky situations. To think it was the first and only time I ever saw him . . .'

Nilsen and Le Fox parted company at Kentish Town underground station on a spring Saturday morning in May, 1982, with a promise to meet again the following Tuesday, an appointment which Le Fox did not keep. But Le Fox did go to the London Hospital in White-chapel Road where allegedly a doctor identified small broken blood vessels in his neck and said, 'Who tried to kill you? We'll have to call the police . . .'

But Le Fox did nothing about it. He knew only too well, he said, how the police regarded homosexuals so he vanished. Only by chance, four weeks after Nilsen was arrested, did Le Fox appear as a witness at Southwark police station on the south side of the River Thames. He had seen an incident outside another hostel.

A police officer picked up the photofit picture and challenged him. As a result, Le Fox was warned that while Nilsen would not be charged with attempting to kill him he might well be called by the prosecution to give evidence of Nilsen's nocturnal behaviour from his position in the pub to his predilection to kill.

Another of Nilsen's casual acquaintances who almost suffered the same fate also did not tell the police of a murderous attempt at the time. He is Paul Nobbs, a mature Polish language student, who comes from a good suburban background, son of a precision engi-neer, of Spring Crofts, a pleasant road on the edge of the 'green belt' at Bushey, Watford, Hertfordshire. What Nobbs had failed at first to volunteer was now amply provided by Nilsen. The two had met in the

Golden Lion in Dean Street where both were 'cruising' in search of a partner.

By both their accounts there was perhaps not a considerable sexual attraction between them, but they were both intelligent enough to find some agreeable subject for conversation, Paul with his devotion to the western Slavonic languages, Dennis with his interest in his own half-Norwegian ancestry. Nilsen was at the time involved heavily in trade union affairs, having been a union representative of the Civil and Public Services Association, and he struck Nobbs as being markedly left of centre.

It was late November, the week beginning Sunday the twenty fifth, and Nilsen was already talking about Christmas. He was going to call on his experiences as an army chef and produce a magnificent curry in a special large saucepan he had bought and serve the meal to his colleagues in the Manpower Services Commission. The saucepan was ideal, Nilsen had said, and as the police were to discover, for a number of other reasons.

Nobbs, by his own admission, had been a practising homosexual 'for the last few years' and knew well the dangers that can befall the unwary being picked up in the street or public houses, invited out, assaulted, beaten up and 'rolled' for money and valuables. But the stranger who said, 'Call me Desi,' appeared more considerate and gentle and of higher intelligence than most gays he had met in such circumstances.

Unlike the other victims who survived the murderous attacks Nobbs did not wake up to find himself with a ligature round his neck, close to blacking out or dying. He woke up and just did not feel himself, a condition he ascribed to the fact that he had drunk too much the previous evening both at the Golden Lion and at Cranley Gardens. He returned to the centre of

London, called at University College Hospital close to the university and asked for a check on his health.

The duty physician looked into Paul's eyes which he thought were 'popping'.

'Undo your shirt, please. Just the top buttons,' said the doctor. He saw a mass of ugly red marks and applied slight pressure to the patient's windpipe. Paul Nobbs winced. 'Mr Nobbs, what were you doing last night?'

'Why do you ask?'

'I think someone has tried to strangle you.'

Paul's eyes must have popped even further when he recalled the evening with Nilsen, returning to Muswell Hill, drinking too much alcohol and falling asleep in the armchair. So Nilsen had tried to strangle him.

Nobbs buttoned his shirt and went away to reflect. He did not advertise his homosexual tendencies and though he was shocked by what he had heard he was also silenced. It would do no good for him to make public that he had been picked up in a public house, returned to the home of another gay, drunk too much, fallen asleep and had to be told by a doctor next day that his host must have tried to asphyxiate him. Paul Nobbs kept his peace, until he read Nilsen had been arrested and he called the Murder Squad.

Nilsen was accurate again, pinpointing the entertainment of Nobbs to the week beginning Sunday, November 25, 1981, seven weeks after he had moved to Cranley Gardens, about four weeks before Christmas.

About that Christmas, the detectives persisted, what did Nilsen use that giant saucepan for apart from making a delicious curry for his colleagues at the Manpower Services Commission? 'Oh, that,' said Nilsen. 'I used that to boil up the remains of some of the victims.'

119

The police may have been unable to find the Japanese, the Chinese, a juvenile and others, but they had Stewart, with his ear-bending story, and now they had the more reserved, intelligent language student Paul Nobbs with so similar a tale that they were bound to charge Nilsen that in addition to murdering so many people, in addition to trying to kill Stewart he had also attempted to murder Paul Nobbs.

Nine

The dossier that was now assembled by Chambers and Jay and the Murder Squad had not only reached gargantuan proportions but it was decorated with so bizarre allegations that they would test the credence of any intelligent reader. Their duty, of course, was to put forward a case which, in the words of the Director of Public Prosecutions, Sir Thomas Hetherington, would stand more than a fifty per cent chance of resulting in criminal conviction.

Detectives were certain of that, but they were also very much aware that they were exposing not only to a future judge and jury but to the largely ignorant public an unacceptable face of society, a garish panorama of permissiveness which led to murder, mass murder. It was only right that criminal behaviour should be exposed, tested in the courts and if found to be true, punished. But what the police were told threatened to have a marked effect on current liberal thought which tolerates homosexuality without approving it. The very much darker side of the gay rights era was about to be exposed to the limelight.

The Director of Public Prosecutions had rightly decided that the jury, faced with allegations of mass murder, must be provided with as many witnesses as would testify to that multiple of killings. It was necessary so that the jury, properly directed by the judge, could weigh up on balance the stories they heard, particularly those of the volatile Douglas Stewart, the more precise Paul Nobbs and even the theatrical Khara Le Fox.

Despite the indulgent attitude towards those who preferred love with their own sex, the so called love that dares not speak its name, there was a danger that a jury of twelve good men and true might be so horrified, so tempted to doubt the extravaganza of homosexual behaviour that they might distrust the whole story. After all, Dennis Nilsen's own story, not to mention that of Stewart, Nobbs, Le Fox and the others had surprised experienced police officers. What would it do to a judicial panel of a dozen ordinary men and women?

But, while the case of Regina v. Nilsen moved slowly through the judicial process to full trial, another violent death came to public attention. The incident concerned, appropriately and accidentally, a visitor from abroad who was befriended by a London resident. The host was Peter Arne, the well know actor, who had appeared in such television series as 'Softly, Softly,' 'The Avengers,' 'The Saint,' and 'Secret Army.' His film credits bore eloquent testimony to his ability as an actor: 'Cockleshell Heroes,' 'Ice Cold in Alex,' 'The Dam Busters,' 'Straw Dogs,' 'Chitty Chitty Bang Bang,' and 'Agatha.' He was rehearsing for the long-running, 'Dr Who' series for television when he met his guest in Hyde Park.

While Nilsen used public houses, Peter Arne, the Battle of Britain fighter pilot, knowledgeable art and antique collector and homosexual, preferred the Serpentine, Rotten Row and the carriageways of London's most famous open acres. There he picked up Guiseppe Perusi, an Italian school teacher, at thirty-two just half Peter Arne's age.

All officialdom really knew was that Arne picked up younger men who were down on their luck and Perusi,

a teacher of handicapped children, a Communist coun-
cillor from Verona, had recently lost faith in women
and had gone on a walking, rambling holiday across
Europe 'to find himself'. Instead, Arne found him and
took him home to his luxurious apartment overlooking
the top people's store, Harrod's.

The Italian who looked like Jesus Christ, with his
long curly hair and beard, carrying a knapsack and
wearing a white safari suit that looked as if he had
slept in it, asked at the block of flats for 'Peter' and was
directed to the actor's front door. Later was heard
coming from the residence the cries, 'oh, oh, oh, oh'.
Someone was trying to shout through the intercom-
munication system to the front door but was being
pulled away from the speaker.

Inside, the actor was being savagely beaten with a
fire log, stabbed in the face, slashed in the neck
producing a torrential haemhorrage from the severed
jugular vein and carotid artery. A wooden stool that
had been used in the assault was also in evidence, but
there was no sign of the Italian. Next day his naked
body, naked but for a woman's headscarf tied round
his neck, the last memento of a female lover, was found
in the River Thames at Wandsworth.

That story of a fatal pick-up in the park by a well
known actor, resulting in the murder of the host and
the suicide of the guest, was told to the Westminster
coroner a few days before Dennis Andrew Nilsen,
author of so many homosexual pick-ups, stood trial at
the Old Bailey. The world, in the relative confines of
the British mind, was probably ready to hear the full
horrendous tale.

Of course, in the true reserved British fashion, the
jury would not be told the whole story. Not only was
it not intended for the prurient, much of it would serve

no judicial purpose in deciding Nilsen's innocence or guilt.

They might not know that while some homosexuals find prostitution a trade that provides not only easy money and sometimes sexual satisfaction, a greater number turn to the business in desperation for the price of a meal, the chance of a bed for the night. Many are not by literal definitio homosexuals – those attracted by members of the same sex – but merely out to earn money, small money at that, or a reward in kind. Many of the unscrupulous have no intention of indulging in any sort of sexual contact. Once they have wormed their way into the company, confidence and front doors of their 'tricks', as they call their customers, they use any wile, force or story, to steal what they can from their victims, safe in the knowledge that the embarrassed victims will not report the incidents to the police. Thus they are 'rolled' in large numbers without the police having any official knowledge of the crimes.

Male prostitution is not just an easy way to bolster the pittance in the pockets of so many, usually what is left from the fortnightly Giro cheques collected by the destitute and unemployed from the Department of Health and Social Security. At least two of Nilsen's fifteen victims fell into this category.

A sexual experience is not essential for the emergence of a homosexual relationship but in the Nilsen calendar it could be found merely in bodily contact, mutual masturbation or fellatio without reaching fruition in buggery, traditionally the word used by those who condemn homosexuality, referred to in the common parlance of gays as 'screwing'. At other times the male prostitutes in Nilsen's company (though his bizarre tastes are by no means unique among his kind) would have to be prepared for anything, or at least

124

know how to avoid what is repugnant to them without endangering their lives.

If only the jury to be empanelled in Regina v. Nilsen belonged to a court of truth, where everything is told, instead of a court of record in which all the court is required to know is the case for the prosecution and the case for the defence. If it were different they might hear one male prostitute who claims to have been possibly the longest standing friend of Nilsen. He gives his name as Martin Hunter-Craig (which he took from a television executive with whom he had an affair as a teenager), his age as twenty-four (with unbecoming modesty), his birthplace as the Midlands and his address as Exeter, Devon, which hides a multitude of accents and covers his tracks when anyone wants to ask him questions.

When eventually interviewed Hunter-Craig claimed that he had lived with Nilsen at both Melrose Avenue and at Cranley Gardens for a period of eleven months. Hunter-Craig met Nilsen at an amusement arcade near Piccadilly Circus.

Nilsen thought, not unnaturally, that since Hunter and Craig are both Scots names, Hunter-hyphen-Craig must also be a fellow Scot, a mistake that the prostitute was only too glad to encourage. After all, any introduction was better than none. He was in the amusement arcade because, like so many others, he had nowhere to go, nowhere to sleep and no money and knew that he could only survive by offering sexual acts for food or cash. That suited Nilsen.

He insisted that Hunter-Craig return to his flat, and later told him that he could stay as long as he liked. After an evening of Nilsen drinking copious quantities of vodka they retired to the two-tier bunk. From that very first night, according to Hunter-Craig, they became very good friends. 'You look so lovely when you wake up,' Nilsen had said to him. 'Come to bed.' Cash changed hands next morning and the impoverished prostitute found he had a free season ticket to a gay bedsitter. He was more than happy to let the affair continue for he remained blissfully unaware of what had happened or what was to happen to the total of fifteen others who were to accept the same hospitality.

The two became very close, Hunter-Craig calling Nilsen 'Desi' and Nilsen calling Hunter-Craig by the nickname, 'Skip', a mocking abbreviation of Skipper given to him by sex-starved sailors, promoting their effeminate companion to the rank of a naval officer.

Although both men found many other partners during the eleven months, the prostitute was not of a jealous disposition. He could carry on his own business with others and always return for a bed for the night providing Nilsen was not otherwise engaged with a lover or, as Hunter-Craig now knows, someone to murder.

The conversation and the behaviour during some weird nights still haunt Hunter-Craig. 'Although Desi remains very special to me, he was really like Dr Jekyll and Mr Hyde, because, I think, of his heavy drinking. Perhaps it's because I don't drink myself that I am still alive. He would drink whole tumblers of spirits, either gin or vodka. And then he would want to act out strange games. For instance, he would play the psychiatrist and I would be the patient, with the object of him insulting me, humiliating me, reducing me to tears until I would submit to sex.'

In another recollection, Hunter-Craig said, 'Nilsen told me that I was the only person who would ever listen to him and that is why he liked me. In my job as a homosexual prostitute I reckon I've seen every trick in the book, but he showed me some more. One of his special sex games was something else. It was called "necrophiliac's revenge". He would play as if he were dead and I would play the part of being alive, literally trying to persuade me to have sex with him as if he was a corpse.

'Once he, even asked me if I fancied the idea of bathing in a bath of blood. I said the whole idea disgusted me. He just gave a crazy sort of laugh, but he did not forget it. He would wait for a moment suitable to him and ask me again. He did it on several occasions.'

Together they watched a television documentary about the Jews in Hitler's concentration camps during the second World War. Nilsen, his companion recalled, laughed when horrific black and white pictures of corpses appeared on the screen. 'He told me how the Nazis used various parts of the bodies of Jews for sexual experiments.' And then came this conversation.

'We should be doing that now with wogs,' Nilsen declared, and, after describing how Nazis bathed in Jewish blood said, 'Would you accept one hundred pounds for a blood bath?'

'No, of course not,' said Hunter-Craig.

'A thousand pounds?'

'No.'

'All I could do was to play the story down and say things like, "What on earth are you going on about, Desi?"

Then he would say, "I just want to know what it would be like. It must be nice to wash in blood." '

Nilsen, according to his permanent guest, was anxious to impress listeners that he was a person of culture, well read, literary and artistic. He was alternately fascinated by Barbara Cartland's pure love stories and by Shakespeare's tragedies. He listened to rock music on his stereo equipment and was always anxious to see any new musical, particularly 'Cats' and

'Jesus Christ Superstar'. Then he would discuss philosophy.

'You know what he said to me once? He said, "Skip, do you think it is possible that Satan is God and that God is really Satan?" I listened but I didn't understand at all.'

There is little doubt that Nilsen had read something of Nietzsche, the German philosopher, ascetic anti-Christ, who produced the theory of the overman, or higher type in society, which the Nazis mistakenly claimed was in their philosophy, too. Nietzsche, though syphilitic, paralytic and insane by any standard at the end of his life, left the world with 'the last man'. Evolution, biological and social, leads to the last man because, 'One still loves one's neighbour and rubs against him, for one needs warmth . . . A little poison now and then: that makes for agreeable dreams. And much poison in the end for an agreeable death . . . One still works, for work is a form of entertainment. But one is careful lest the entertainment be too harrowing. One no longer becomes poor or rich: both require too much exertion. Who still wants to rule? Who obey? Both require too much exertion . . . No shepherd and one herd! Everybody wants the same, everybody is the same: whoever feels differently goes voluntarily into a madhouse.'

The quotation from 'Zarathustra's Prologue' by Friedrich Nietzsche sounded like some of Nilsen's verbal ventures into philosophy, but he believed the herd was going nowhere because it did need an overman or superman and not a last man. Nilsen dreamed of overturning what Nietzsche thought was inevitable which is why he turned to the Nazi version of the philosopher's work.

'He was very much into things like that,' said Hunter-Craig. 'He had all these cassettes with recordings of the Nazi rallies, songs and speeches, including some by Adolf Hitler. He used to play them and ask me, "Do you not feel a sense of power when you hear that man speak?" There was one particularly favourite tape he played. It sounded like an old German news bulletin with a very smooth English voice-over producing a simultaneous translation. Desi told me that it was a news report of some Nazi officials who had been discovered to be homosexuals and Hitler had them killed.'

It would take more than an admittedly observant friend like Hunter-Craig to decide in which order Nilsen really had his loves and his hates and which were which, homosexuals and Nazis, the haves and the have-nots, men and women, pigeons and people, soldiers, policemen and civil servants. Nilsen, at best, was a talker, and who could say whether he had a blood lust which he took from the Nazis, and being a homosexual was the only way he could meet and pick up human beings to satisfy that primitive appetite? Hunter-Craig? Blood lust? 'All I know is that at Cranley Gardens I was never allowed in the spare room in the front of the house where the police told me they found two plastic sacks full of human remains and three boiled skulls.'

Once, Hunter-Craig remembered, he was looking for washing up liquid under the kitchen sink when Nilsen screamed at him 'Don't look there again or I'll kick your head in.'

Hunter-Craig almost accused Nilsen of cannibalism. 'He used to cook. He was a good cook. But sometimes he wouldn't let me into the kitchen. He would have soup on occasions. Once it was really horrible. It tasted like bad meat. Another time he made a pie and it was literally putrid. It was meat but it tasted like yoghurt. I told him that I couldn't eat it. "It smells like vomit,"

I said. He looked very uncomfortable, snatched the plates away and said he would speak to the butcher. That time he gave the remains to the dog.'

Which jury would believe that? Before Hunter-Craig is dismissed as a fantasist it is Nilsen's own confession that he dismembered his victims, boiled them in the saucepan which he had brought originally for the curry party for his colleagues at the Manpower Services Commission. Is it so far fetched, so far beyond comprehension that such a man would talk about bathing in blood, and if so that such a man would serve human remains to a guest? Sooner or later someone would have to try at least to fathom Nilsen's apparently tortured and unchained mind.

For the time being there was only the word of witnesses like Martin Hunter-Craig. He was invited to explain the breadth of Nilsen's sexual proclivities. Nilsen himself only confided that he had picked up a Swiss nurse. They met, he said, in a similar way to that in which he met his homosexual victims. He took her home, he said, had sexual intercourse with her and parted next day, never to see her again. 'That is the only woman I ever slept with,' Nilsen declared, totally ignorant of her name. Nilsen's mother confessed that as far as she knew Nilsen had only taken his own sister, Sylvia, to any party and that was natural. She knew of no girl friends with whom he might have had sex.

Hunter-Craig, on the other hand, had a far more singular version of Nilsen's friendship with a woman. Nilsen used to speak to her at pre-arranged times from the coin operated telephone in Melrose Avenue. 'If I was with him I used to have to wait outside the house. He didn't like me being around at that time and he usually got rid of me on one pretext or another. You know, he would send me round to the off licence to buy a bottle of spirits. I remember at least five occasions when he spoke to her. Each time for some reason he got very angry. You could hear him shouting inside the house.

'It was Desi who told me her name. I asked him if she meant anything to him. He just laughed and said, "No way," But there was something strange about his answer. He went on to say, "Do you ever get the urge to hurt someone? That's how I feel about that woman." I asked again what she meant to him and Desi said, "I have got to get on with her, that's all." He said she lived in America, but sometimes came to England.

'She rang twice at Cranley Gardens when I was there. Once I answered. She seemed to be calling from abroad, you know you can tell from the sound on the line. But she sounded English. She had no accent, none that I can identify. She was not American or Canadian. All she said was, "Can I speak to Mr Nilsen?" '

Because Hunter-Craig remembers another time when 'I met him at the Job Centre in Denmark Street and I was supposed to be going home with him. But he offered me twenty pounds to stay away. He said his sister was coming to stay and it would be embarrassing to have me around. I thought it was odd even at the time because he had always said that he didn't get on with his sister. They hadn't seen each other for five years, he said.

'Well, I went to stay with him after that weekend on the Monday and you could tell there had been a woman there. It was all clean and tidy. I told him, teasingly, that I didn't believe that it was his sister. I said it was obviously another man. Then I said I thought it was this girl. He got very angry with me. She somehow seemed to have some sort of influence on him. She was able to dominate him.'

Hunter-Craig told all this to the police but they, knowing that Nilsen's sister, Sylvia, is in Canada and is not on frequent speaking terms with her brother, dismissed the story as a total fabrication. The male prostitute, though, was not to be put off his theory about the mystery woman.

Police similarly dismissed the story that a woman actually telephoned while they were clearing Cranley Gardens. A police constable is supposed to have answered the pay-phone on the first floor landing.

'Hello,' he said.

'Can I speak to Des?'

'Er, sorry. No. He's not here.'

'Well, I've just landed at London Heathrow from New York and I want to see him if I can.'

'The best thing you can do, miss, is to come down here and go to Hornsey police station and I'll sort it out for you down there.'

The police version is that no such call was made. No such call was recorded. No police constable with the slightest training would take it on himself, during a murder investigation, to answer such a call or to carry on that conversation. He would ask the caller for her number, ask her to hold the line open, seek a superior officer who would in turn ensure that she was picked up and escorted to a police station for questioning. In any event the woman did not arrive, has never been seen, and the police version stands up to any investigation.

But before Hunter-Craig is dismissed from the scene, as if his realm was one of fantasy, what would the police make of the story of another male prostitute who could at least strengthen part of Hunter-Craig's evidence? Peter Lamont was important in more than one respect. He was another Scot, once fostered out to parents in Dundee, and twenty-one years of age when he came to London and paired up with Billy Sutherland, one of Nilsen's future victims, to work the Shepherds Market area in Mayfair in competition with the hordes of pestering female prostitutes there. He got on well with Sutherland.

Then Lamont, tattooed with his trade name, 'Elsie', went to the Golden Lion and met Nilsen. 'One night I was sitting in the Royal Box with the other Queens at the Golden Lion, looking for a trick, you know, and this Nilsen comes up. I asked him if he wanted to do business. He said he did and we went back in a taxi to Melrose Avenue. I don't remember at all what it was like there. I've been in so many bedrooms, they've just become a blur over the years. He was drinking pretty heavily, I remember that.

'Well, I was with him for a total of three hours on that occasion. We had sex. He screwed me, you know. I didn't screw him. I'm a woman, not a lesbian, dear, and afterwards he insisted that I pissed all over him. We call it "water sports" in our game, sometimes if we are posh it's "golden rain". I said I couldn't do it. So he said that if it made it any easier then he would run the kitchen tap. But I still refused.

'He then suggested a bit of bondage, that he should tie me up. I had no intention of letting him do that so I refused again. Nilsen never ever threatened me, but he had those sort of eyes that look straight through you. You know what I mean. I felt at the time that he seemed quite capable of doing exactly what he wanted to do. In all our games he insisted that he was the master and I had to do what he wished. He asked me to stay the night, but I had friends to meet at Heaven, you know the gay disco down in Villiers Street. So he paid me thirty pounds and turned away to go to the toilet. That gave me the opportunity to go, so I rushed out and caught a taxi back to Charing Cross.

'The second time I met him was about four months later in the Golden Lion. I was with Billy Sutherland and I was skint. All I could do was nurse half a pint of bitter all night and hope for a punter. Well, this Nilsen comes in so I proposition him there and then. He agreed to do business but I didn't want to go all the way to his place so we went to a hotel near Capital Radio.

'We didn't have full sex that time and he only paid me twenty pounds. Again I left when he went to the toilet and got a taxi back to the Golden Lion. On neither occasion did he threaten me, but he always looked a bit odd. He had those strange, quite evil eyes and I never felt really comfortable in his presence. I was always glad to get back to something straight in the market, if you know what I mean.'

The rhetorical question was by then lost on the police. They had heard more than enough and besides Nilsen was safely incarcerated in Her Majesty's prison, Brixton, awaiting trial. They had enough on him, as they say. He could consult anyone he liked, receive any visitors he liked, but their investigation was complete.

Ten

Brixton Prison has the smell of eggs and bacon and human waste, not only at 6.45 a.m., the slopping out time every morning. It lingers in the fetid air and will do as long as Brixton remains the principal remand prison in London handling sixty thousand prisoners a year in outdated buildings in an outmoded system. Dennis Andrew Nilsen was one of them but to Brixton he was B62006, even before his trial a prisoner without a name, without a cell to himself.

Brixton Prison was built in 1819 as the Surrey House of Correction and has been added to over the years until it is now a jumble of buildings within an overcrowded perimeter, giving the impression of being terribly restricted and enclosed. Flowers and shrubs have been planted in an attempt to brighten the place, but the backdrop and skyline of London brick wherever one looks gives the place an air of drabness which has a depressing effect on both those who visit it and those who live in it, either as prisoners or prison staff.

At any one time there are eight hundred prisoners, the majority of whom have to be taken once a week to some magistrates' court only to be remanded in custody for another week and returned to the prison. There are eighty to one lavatory. Then they queue for breakfast from trolleys and take the food back to their cells to eat, idle their time or await transportation to court.

Those to go to remand hearings are checked in three

times, out three times, once to check their valuables, once to check their bedding and once to make sure they are clearly identified, for more than one prisoner has switched places with another, arrived in court and declared from the dock that they are dealing with the wrong person. Farcical though the system and sometimes the behaviour may be it is not a laughing matter for those who value their liberty and who, under the rule that a man is innocent until proved guilty, must be imprisoned for long periods before they can be tried.

Prison authorities believe it is better for men to share cells with prisoners of their own choosing if only there is sufficient room. Nilsen was to find the system repulsive and the thought of mixing with a high proportion of drunks, drug addicts, mentally ill and known, if not high risk and violent, criminals appalling. Not surprisingly he rebelled. At Hornsey police station, in the relative comfort of a police station cell, he had no grumble. Investigating officers had treated him with uncommon and unfailing courtesy. Throughout the long interviews there had been breaks for coffee in the morning, tea in the afternoon, statutory lunch breaks and supper breaks and no late night questioning. While on one of Nilsen's weekly visits to court to be remanded, his solicitor at the time, Mr Ronald Moss, said, 'I am authorized by my client to say that since his arrest he has been treated well by the police and has received regular visits by a divisional police surgeon.'

But when the questioning was over and he was sent to Brixton that all changed.

At first the authorities saw no reason why Nilsen should be treated any differently from any other prisoner. He was in no dangers, as a child batterer may be, nor was he violent towards others. He might, of course, try to escape, since his prospects at the hands of a judge and jury on a mass murder charge were grim. So he was told to wear the traditional blue prison battledress. Who knows, if he remained in Brixton long enough, he might earn a red arm band to show that he was to be trusted with certain supervisory duties over other prisoners?

At the next court hearing, Mr Moss was instructed to make another protest. Nilsen told him, 'I have not tried to escape, nor will I, but I am not going to wear prison uniform.' Mr Moss told the magistrates who nodded sympathetically because while they believe a man is innocent and should not be identified by uniform until guilty they have no jurisdiction at all over the prison administration. That is a matter for the Home Office.

Nilsen on one occasion used the ploy of discharging his legal aid certificate to obtain better conditions. That meant, technically, he would dispense with his solicitor, who was to be paid from legal aid funds, and defend himself. Not being a lawyer he would fight the system by demanding every entitlement due to a prisoner, every document – important and significant or not – and throw the establishment legal arrangements into disarray. In the end, he was not only moved to the airy, modern prison hospital wing but everything around him seemed to change for the better.

At least Nilsen thought so. Into the hospital wing came a friend, a fellow rebel, David Martin, for a short time Britain's most wanted criminal. He impressed Dennis Nilsen with his record, with his stories, his drift into petty crime, graduating from a detention centre, then to a twenty-one month sentence and then to an eight year sentence for forgery and fraud.

Martin had befriended a locksmith whose tuition helped him master the secrets of breaking locks, including twice escaping from a prison van, and then he became interested in guns. He needed guns to prove he was a criminal and had the utmost contempt for authority. He used the guns while stealing equipment to cash in on the growing criminal piracy of commercially made video films. When confronted by a police constable at a colour film laboratory in Marylebone, London, he shot the officer in the groin.

Police traced him to a London flat and them ambushed him when he met his girl friend in a Hampstead cafe, but not before someone who resembled him and travelled in a mini-car with his girl friend was shot by mistake. When Martin was ambushed he darted down the London underground system at Hampstead station, running through the darkened tunnel, avoiding trains, all the way to Belsize Park station until the police had sealed off the northern line section.

The sheer bravado of it all endeared Martin to Nilsen, and the fact that Martin was a transvestite bonded their friendship even closer. In fact when Nilsen used the device of discharging his legal aid certificate by dismissing his solicitor he was merely imitating a stratagem of Martin's. Together they worked on how Nilsen should organize his defence and that consultation led Nilsen to dismiss Mr Moss, his solicitor, who had instructed Mr Anthony Powell, Q.C., to appear for Nilsen at his trial. Instead, Nilsen engaged Martin's solicitor, who instructed the same counsel who appeared for Martin, Mr Ivan Lawrence, Q.C.

Nilsen, in his talks with Martin, was encouraged to show his rebellion more openly. Otherwise, said Martin, 'no one will ever respect you.' Nilsen obliged by throwing the contents of his chamber pot over three prison officers and during the scuffle which ensued lost a tooth. For that he was sentenced to solitary

confinement and to twenty-eight days loss of privi-
leges, a punishment which deprived him of Martin's
much needed company.

Nilsen had long finished that punishment when his
'only friend', as he called him, was removed from his
company. An Old Bailey judge told Martin, 'Those
who carry loaded guns in order to shoot their way out
of impending arrest must expect very severe sentences
indeed and that's what are you going to get.' He was
sentenced to a total of twenty-five years in prison.

His former companion in the prison hospital wing
could not help wondering if a prisoner was given
twenty-five years for shooting at a policeman and
wounding him what would the courts give an ex-
policeman who had boasted of sixteen murders?

Nilsen was still pondering that question when he
came to trial, but meanwhile his stay in Brixton Prison
had taken a toll of him both mentally and physically.
Observers who saw him at the magistrates' court, at
the Central Criminal Court, when he applied to change
his lawyers, noted the change. When he appeared at
Highgate Magistrates' Court on February 12, 1983, to
answer the charge of murder for the first time he
looked noticeably taller than the detective at his side,
showed off his twelve stone and would have looked a
formidable figure if he was still a policeman and in
uniform. He looked arrogantly and coldly at the mag-
istrate who glanced at the clerk to the court as if he
was wondering whether he would be attacked. Now
on September 19, at the Central Criminal Court, seven
months later, he looked drawn and haggard, his arms
poking out punily from his shirt sleeves.

Since he left the army poetry had been his favourite
means of expressing himself to himself. He had given
pieces to friends, like this passage for Hunter-Craig,
the fantasist:

Born with nothing,
Being Nothing,
Ending up Nothing.
Very, very lonely.
Somebody Save Us.

To Douglas Bence, co-author of this volume, he wrote, 'I'm a poor performance poet. Have you noticed that good art seems to be born out of the personal emotional pain of the artist. I have written some poetry of no consequence between February and today's date. (August 10, 1983). I just try and express myself this way without reference to popularity. I produce pieces spontaneously and rarely work to refine or correct anything that I do.'

His motivation was no different to many other writers who do not have to earn a living from their work. It was to 'please and express' himself, ignoring 'strict, acceptable and correct formats' and always refusing to 'play to the crowd'. He admitted that most of what he had done, in a poetical context, was 'probably thoroughly bad' and that he ought to stick to 'writing and filing dull Civil Service reports.'

In prose he said, 'I have tried to keep busy writing pages and pages of notes. These are past reflections on my life and on this case. Up until the end of June I kept a complete record of my time in Brixton. I was fairly meticulous in my observations and life still holds many surprises for me. The papers have been locked in a bank vault to prepare a detailed and accurate history of the case and the social background to it. I have given all my notes freely on the pre-condition that neither I nor my family will receive any payment whatsoever for such a serious and tragic matter as my central case.'

Nilsen was writing then in the vein of the serious thinker he wished to be thought, although he took an omnibus Shakespearean volume to court his only known contribution to the work of the Bard was his mock Shakespearean 'Bordello, the Moor of Bromley,' with the credit line that 'the good fairy appears by kind permission of the Willesden Police.'

Act IV, Scene 8 has this 'Scene: A gay day near a bog in Brixton.

SIR CYRIL SMALLPIECE:
> Does now the Queen oft-times recall
> The pleasure once of holding balls
> For squires and hangers on I think
> And Dukes and Earls in shocking pink.

QUEEN BELLA XXCVIDLX:
> I still have fondest memories clear
> Of Cheaper fags and bodied beer
> I used to feel a little queer.
> Pray send for Butch Bordello.

COURT TRUMPETER:
> I will summon with my brass
> To get Bordello off his ass.

And he signed this and much of his work 'F' or 'Friedal Mokesheim' which was, strangely, the name of a branch of his father's family whom he had never met. He took it from the one time he heard from his father – posthumously. Olav Nilsen married four times, first to Dennis's mother, Elizabeth Whyte, in 1942, then to two Norwegians, one of whom died, and then to an English woman in Oxfordshire. He then adopted the name Mokesheim, which was that of his mother's family, and which he gave to his fourth wife. He then moved to Ghana where he managed a fishing firm for a Norwegian company, holding the post until he died, Mr Mokesheim, on August 20, 1973. Dennis was not told of his father's death until the following January.

The estate of the man who abandoned his Scottish family was substantial. Dennis's share was £1,400.

Poems, written at the time, early 1974, all carried the Mokesheim name. It may have been a fancy, an affectation, a piece of tomfoolery to impress others, to invite the question, 'why do you do that, Dennis?' Certainly no one around him in Brixton could fathom him, not even David Martin. The psychiatrists might discover something closer to the truth about his imperfect mind.

Nilsen was to be seen by two psychiatrists. The first, called by the prosecution, was Dr Paul Bowden, consultant forensic psychiatrist, of the Maudsley Hospital, London, and later, after protest by Nilsen, Dr MacKeith, a Dublin psychiatrist who had also practised at the Maudsley, and Dr Patrick Gallwey, forensic psychiatrist at the Maudsley and Bethlem Hospitals. Henry Maudsley, who lived from 1835 to 1918, was an English physician who devoted himself, soon after qualifying as a doctor, to the study of mental illness. Through his writings he exerted great influence on contemporary psychiatric thought. He believed that mental diseases were due to diseases of the brain, and that it was more important to examine our tendency to contract diseases than the mental symptoms of insanity with the emphasis on heredity or 'inborn structure' of human beings.

He sought a more enlightened policy in the early treatment of mental disorder and desired to see minute systematic research into the heredity and pathology of mental disease. He therefore offered a large sum of money to the London County Council (predecessor of the Greater London Council) for the creation of a psychiatric hospital which should be a medical school of the university, a centre for research and a clinic for the individual treatment of early mental disorder in out-patients as well as in-patients. The Maudsley Hospital was the outcome although Maudsley himself died before the building was opened.

The position of the Maudsley and its reasonable distance from Brixton Prison has guaranteed the availability of much-needed psychiatrists to examine and report upon the mental state of those awaiting trial or sentence. Even the Chief Inspector of Her Majesty's Prisons, Mr Bill Brister, who is highly critical of Brixton as a remand prison, says, 'Brixton has a substantial hospital and a comparatively large medical staff to cater both for the physical needs of patients and for their assessment for psychiatric reports . . . The psychiatric experience of the senior members of the medical team, together with the consultants who attend on a sessional basis, provided a most sophisticated psychiatric assessment service. We were well satisfied with the quality of the advice given to the courts.'

But what can the courts do with such psychiatric assessments?

While Nilsen was awaiting trial it was regarded as strange that a judge in one London court sent a persistent car thief to see a psychiatrist rather than a prison governor. Since the thief did not steal any other kind of property in his career it seems an admirable attempt to solve the pattern of crime and help the criminal but hardly a pioneering effort in 1983. Similarly the prosecution in Regina v. Nilsen decided quite properly at an early stage that the judge in his case, if not the jury as well, would require a psychiatric assessment of the prisoner. Dr Bowden was appointed to provide that report. But while the State, through the legal aid system, would pay for Nilsen to be independently defended by the lawyers of his choice it would not at first pay for him to have independent psychiatric consideration. Until he protested, and Dr McKeith was appointed by his legal advisers.

The dilemma does not end there. When the psychiatrists have spoken, a judge has four ways in which he can dispose of a mass murderer or other criminal who is clearly a psychiatric case. They are by the use of the McNaghten Rules, by sections 60 or 65 of the Mental Health Act, by treatment as a condition of probation under section 4 of the Criminal Justice Act, or by declaring the prisoner to be unfit to plead due to a mental disorder.

Now the McNaghten Rules were introduced 140 years ago. Daniel McNaghten, a Glaswegian wood turner, thought that the Victorian Prime Minister, Sir Robert Peel, was persecuting him. Then he confused Peel with the Premier's secretary, Edward Drummond. So, on January 20, 1843, he shot Drummond dead. He was brought to trial on a charge of murder at the Central Criminal Court but was acquitted on the grounds of insanity.

The outcry that followed was so great that the House of Lords was persuaded to ask the judges of the time a series of questions on the subject of insanity, an unusual procedure which resulted in the McNaghten Rules. The answers given by the judges was summarized: 'We submit our opinion to be that the jury ought to be told in all cases that every man is to be presumed to be sane and to possess a sufficient degree of reason to be responsible for his crimes, until the contrary be proved to their satisfaction, and that to establish a defence on the grounds of insanity it must be clearly proved that, at the time of committing the act, the accused was labouring under such defect of reason, from disease of the mind, as not to know the nature or the quality of the act he was doing, or, if he did know it, that he did not know he was doing what was wrong.'

The rules were the subject of immediate controversy. Firstly it was unusual, if not unique, to provide a set of rules, not connected with a specific case but to be applied generally, on the subject of guilt or innocence, sanity or insanity. Those rules were to apply to all future questions of insanity before the courts. Maudsley, who gave his name to the hospital, complained that the rules dealt only with knowledge and intellect to the exclusion of feelings and will power. More fundamentally, an accused person was expected to claim that he was sane or insane, and whichever he chose, to argue presumably sanely to convince a jury of his state of mind. A sane man might convince a jury either way but it would be hard for an insane man to persuade a jury of anything.

Despite that criticism from the outset, all those years ago, the McNaghten Rules remain today the supreme test of insanity in English law, in most states of the United States of America, throughout the English-speaking world and in other countries where English-speaking administration has given way to more local control. All this is despite the fact that the Rules were written some sixty years before the psychiatrists like Freud, Jung, Kraepelin, Blueler and others began to challenge the concept of insanity. Eighty years on from them the same test applies even though the very word 'insanity' has no medical meaning, having been sub-divided into so many states of responsibility. It only has a judicial meaning and an outdated one at that.

Alternatively, a defendant could plead not guilty to murder but guilty to manslaughter by virtue of the fact that he was suffering at the time from diminished responsibility. This plea, adopted from an old Scottish concept, means (under the Homicide Act of 1957) that if suffering from such an abnormality of mind as to impair substantially his mental responsibility for killing somebody, he shall not be convicted of murder. If such a plea is successful the verdict must be manslaughter, which frees the judge from the responsibility of sending the prisoner to life imprisonment or similar mandatory sentence.

The judge, in both murder and manslaughter cases, can invoke the Mental Health Act, but certain requirements have to be met, and it involves the whole question of 'mad or bad.' Section 60 of the Act allows the judge to make a hospital order if he considers it more appropriate than prison on account of 'mental disorder,' which covers a multitude of conditions, mental illness, psychopathy and subnormality. Two medical certificates are required, one of which must be from a doctor recognized for the purpose by the local authority. One of the doctors must attend to give evidence. It must be stated that treatment is required and that the patient will be susceptible to it, and why hospitalization is required. In the case of psychopathy a persistent disorder of the mind must be established.

But the system is full of Catch 22 situations. Some hospitals are criticized because they take advantage of the rule that they must tell the judge that they are willing to accept the prisoner. They refuse on the grounds that the prisoner is unlikely to respond to treatment. In that case many chronic psychotics would be refused treatment and in the case of psychopaths none at all, for there is no known treatment for the great majority of psychopaths, nor is there any evidence that psychopaths respond to treatments which have been devised. All this has been confirmed by successive authorities, by practising psychiatrists, by a government working party on secure mental hospitals like Broadmoor, Rampton and Moss Side and by the last report of the late Lord Butler's Committee on Mentally Abnormal Offenders.

Judges, trying to meet the demand that murderers must be removed from society, have to weigh the advantages to both society and the prisoner between prison and hospital. They take the view in many cases – some say too many – that prison amounts to treatment in certain cases especially of course of subnormality. Prisons have hospital wings and have psychiatrists so a subnormal prisoner is being treated without going to a hospital outside the prison service.

Of course, the fear is that a murderer and particularly a mass murderer if sent to a hospital might find it more easy to escape, and there is a great risk that under Section 60 the doctor, a consultant on the medical staff, will discharge the patient after too short a time. If the prisoner is released and then murders again, as has happened so often, there is a public outcry.

Most psychiatrists, including Dr Bowden, do not believe that these patients who are freed to kill again are sufficiently large in numbers to present a threat to society or the system. They are less than ten per cent, although outside the psychiatric system there will always be an argument that one murderer, let alone one per cent or ten per cent is more than enough.

To avoid this situation and curb too liberally minded or enthusiastic psychiatrists the court has the right to invoke Section 65 of the Act. This is an order for a limited or for an indefinite period, and while it is in force, the patient can only be allowed out of the hospital grounds, given leave, or discharged, with the consent of the Home Secretary. Some experts, and they include lawyers and judges, not to mention policemen and authors, are under the impression that the Home Secretary does just what the doctors tell him to. In fact doctors can only advise on the length of the order under this section. They have no power to recommend it.

So while under Section 60 a patient can appeal to a Mental Health Tribunal like any other non criminal patient, under Section 65 he can only do so with the consent of the Home Secretary, to whom the recommendation goes.

There is a further catch in that while a Section 60 recommendation must state that Broadmoor, say, is willing to take him no such provision is made about whether they will accept him under the more restrictive Section 65. This is a serious omission. A hospital might be willing to take a patient whom it is free to keep in or let out without too much trouble, but it would be more reluctant to take a prisoner for an indefinite time over which it had much less control.

Apply all this to Nilsen and the question remains: is he mad or bad? Should he be sent to prison, obviously for a very long time, with a recommendation to the Home Secretary that he serve not less than so many years? Multiple murders usually invite recommendations that they serve the rest of their useful life in person and a recommendation that 37-year-old Nilsen should stay in prison until he is at least sixty-five, a total of 28 years, would not be out of the question. The sentences are usually in five year periods so he could expect to go down for 25 or 30 years.

If he is bad?

What if he is mad?

Psychopathy comes from the Greek words for mind, *psyche* and for disease, *pathos*. A psychopath is one whose behaviour is abnormal and may be antisocial. He is generally someone with a psychopathic personality, outwardly normal but with a potential for abnormal conduct. That would fit so many people. Certainly a civil servant who goes to the office from Monday to

148

Friday and works from 9 a.m. until 5 p.m. is outwardly normal but one who goes to public houses to pick up strangers, homosexual or not, and takes them home and strangles them has more than a potential for abnormal conduct.

Dr Bowden, Dr McKeith and later Dr Gallwey were to look for some more accurate diagnosis of Nilsen's mind. For Nilsen seems to have several mental conditions, the symptoms of which occur in varying combinations and with varying degrees of intensity. That can be a classic case of schizophrenia, the split mind, but that condition has its own subdivisions. There is the simple schizophrenic whose interests and relations with other people and other subjects are insidiously reduced to zero; the hebephrenic with his shallow and inappropriate responses to questions or other people's behaviour, with foolish or bizarre actions of his own, delusions and hallucinations; the catatonic who is mute or adopts physically statuesque poses, inactivity followed by excessive impulsive, unpredictable speech and motions; and the paranoid type.

The paranoid schizophrenic, who usually develops later in life, often from the mid thirties, is characterized by unrealistic behaviour, illogical thinking, with delusions of persecution or of grandeur, and often has hallucinations. Did Nilsen, between the ages of 34 and 37, embark on a pattern of unrealistic behaviour, believing that he was the sole arbiter of whether his victims were nonentities or not and whether they should live or die? It seems illogical, to say the least, that a civil servant, with the rank of executive officer, earning £7,000 a year, should think that he had such power. As for grandeur, his whole approach to strangers seems to have been that he was more intelligent and cleverer than they. As for persecution, he did have to bear throughout his life the indelible memory that his father had abandoned him, among the whole family, that he was by nature a loner and so often friendless, and that he was always deserving of better than he achieved or was given.

Over-riding these matters is the fact that he is a homosexual, which the psychiatrists are bound to take into account. Some people consider that homosexuality is a personality disorder. Homosexual patterns, contrary to popular modern belief, very seldom develop on the basis of a biological failure. The idea that a gay is that way inclined because he has too small a penis, or only because of some chromosomic deficiency, belongs to old wives' tales and amateur sociology.

Most homosexuals develop their homosexuality when they cannot get on with their parent. (Since homosexuality applies to both men and women the son cannot acquire a wholesome identification with the father and the daughter cannot obtain a proper relationship with her mother). Since Nilsen never knew his father he could not build as he grew up a reasonable rapport with Mr Nilsen.

Some families tolerate, and by mischance, encourage homosexuality by stopping children having any contact with the opposite sex and somehow, not necessarily in words, stop them getting sexual gratifications through members of the same sex. Nilsen's family, although not regular churchgoers, were very religious on the mother's side. 'No washing on Sundays,' said Nilsen's mother. And, in the confines of Fraserburgh the opportunities for misbehaviour (as his mother would put it) were few with other boys or girls.

Nilsen was not an easy patient-prisoner to assess psychiatrically. He seemed perpetually on the edge of violence in Brixton which culminated in the chamber pot assault. He had lost weight, frequently found himself in such a state that he declared he was unable to keep appointments with those who were trying to help him, people such as Mr Moss, his original solicitor, and although he could not actually refuse he did not always want to see Dr Bowden. On one occasion he referred to the prosecution psychiatrist as 'Groucho Marx' because of his dark moustache. Another time it was 'that f.... shrink.' So he demanded his own independent psychiatrist, Dr McKeith.

Both Dr Bowden and Dr McKeith are well aware of the efforts still being made in medicine to show that homosexuality can be cured. This cure is not for those who marry and have children to try to prove that they are normal, but for those who can be persuaded that they are not proud of their homosexual perversion but anxious to change their character and move towards normal sexual enjoyment. This – when it was put to Nilsen – carried with it the necessary condition that he had inner guilt feelings amenable to treatment. That treatment would have to be voluntary with an active cooperation and wish to change. He would have to abandon his homosexual status as a weapon in the perpetual fight against family, friends, colleagues and other non-gay associates whom he blamed for his condition.

Having completed their assessments the psychiatrists closed their files and followed police to the Central Criminal Court for the astonishing case of Regina v. Nilsen.

Eleven

The Old Bailey has lost much of its magic and drama. Long gone by a century are the public hangings which brought out the beast in the crowds of watchers. Long gone are the processions of crimson and ermine gowned judges carrying their nosegays to ward off jail fever. Long gone are the theatrical counsel who sent guilty men to freedom and people of likely innocence to the gallows. No longer do the ushers cry, 'O Yea, O Yea, all manner of persons who have anything to do with the Lord Justices of the Assize of Oyer and Terminer and General Gaol Delivery, draw near and give your attention . . .' It's all more prosaic nowadays.

But occasionally, and very occasionally, there comes to the Central Criminal Court, to give it its proper name – Old Bailey is merely the name of the street, and the street took its name from the old wall of the city – a *cause célèbre* which attracts world-wide attention. Such a case came up before His Honour Mr Justice Croom Johnson at 10.30 a.m. on Monday, October 24, 1983, in the celebrated No. 1 Court of the complex. No one will pretend that truth cannot escape the prying eyes, sharp ears and forensic intelligence to be found in such a place. But no one knew for certain what the judge or jury or counsel or public inside and out would make of Regina v. Nilsen, and particularly of Nilsen himself.

He came up from the cells to the dock, prim and proper, looking like a bank clerk on his day off. He wore his hair a shade longer than was proper for the prototype but he was a caricature of the civil servant behind the desk, bespectacled and precise. The light-grey tweed jacket, dark trousers and ankle-length zip-up boots were necessary to show that he was not going to work that day.

It was his blue day, the pale blue eyes emphasizing the blue of his shirt and the blue and white spotted tie at his throat. Occasionally he would clasp and unclasp his hands and was content at his own account of what had happened, but edgy, even upset, when a witness here or a witness there told a version which he did not accept. Then he would pull out his cheap Bic ballpoint and scribble hasty notes to his lawyers below.

Forensic tricks were out. He was asked if his name was Dennis Andrew Nilsen. He said, 'That is correct.' He was asked how he pleaded to the murders of:

Kenneth James Ockenden on a date in December, 1979.

Martin Brandon Duffey between May 16 and 19, 1980.

William David Sutherland between July 1 and October 31, 1980.

Malcolm Barlow between September 17 and 20, 1981.

John Peter Howlett on a date in March, 1982.

Stephen Neil Sinclair between January 31 and February 2, 1983.

He was further charged with the attempted murders of:

Douglas Stewart between November 9 and 12, 1980.

Paul Nobbs between November 22 and 25, 1981.

He pleaded Not Guilty to every charge.

For, as Mr Allan Green, counsel for the Crown, told the jury of eight men and four women, they would have to decide, after guidance by the judge on what is the law, whether Nilsen is guilty of murder as the

Crown claimed or only guilty of manslaughter because of diminished responsibility as the defence claimed. He would outline the prosecution's case. Then they would hear Mr Ivan Lawrence, Q.C., M.P., put the case for the defence. It was their duty to listen to the facts and decide.

The facts? Well they heard from Nilsen's own mouth and pen this astonishing explanation:

'Unscrambling behaviour (Sexual depression?)

'I guess that I may be a creature – a creature psychopath – who, when in a loss of rationality situation lapses into temporarily a destructive psychopath, a condition induced by rapid and heavy ingestion of alcohol. At the subconscious root lies a sense of total isolation and a desperate search for a sexual identity. I have experienced transitory (sic) sexual relationships with both males and females before my first killing. After this event I was incapable of any intercourse. I felt repelled by myself and, as stated, have had no experience of sexual penetration for some years.

'In a society of labels it is convenient for me to let others believe that I am a homosexual. I enjoy the social company of both men and women, but prefer to drink socially with men.

'I am not in sympathy with the state of women who are the worse for drink.

'God only knows what thoughts go through my mind when it is captive within a destructive binge. Maybe the cunning, stalking killer instinct is the only single concentration released from a mind which in that state knows no morality. It may be the perverted overkill of my need to help people – victims who I decide to release quickly from the slings and arrows of their outrageous fortune, pain and suffering.

'There is no disputing the fact that I am a violent killer under certain circumstances.

'The victim is the dirty platter after the feast and the washing up is a clinical ordinary task. It would be better if my reason for killing could be clinically defined – i.e. robbery, jealousy, hate, revenge, sex, blood, lust or sadism.

'But it's none of these. Or it could be the subconscious outpouring of all the primitive instincts of primeval man. Could it be the case of individual exhaltation of beating the system and the need to beat and confound it time and time again?

'It amazes me that I have no tears for these victims. I have no tears for myself or those bereaved by my actions. Am I a wicked person, constantly under pressure, who just cannot cope with it, who escapes to reap revenge against society through a haze of a bottle of spirits? But maybe it's because I was just born an evil man.

'Living with so much violence and death, I've not been haunted by the souls and ghosts of the dead, leading me to believe that no such fictional phenomena has, does or will ever exist.

'Memories of man's best friend, i.e. my dog, are already a little faded.

'In the normal course of my life I feel I had abnormal powers of mental rationality and morality. When under pressure of work and extreme pain of social loneliness and utter misery I am drawn compulsively to a means of temporary escape from reality. This is achieved by taking increased draughts of alcohol and plugging into stereo music which mentally removes me to a high plane of ecstasy, joy and tears. This is a totally emotional experience.

'This glorious experience and feeling is conjured up in this manner. I relive experiences from childhood to the present – taking out the bad bits.

'When I take alcohol I see myself drawn along and

moved out of my isolated prison flat. I bring (with me) people who are not always allowed to leave me because I want them to share my experiences and high feeling. I still do not know the engine of my performance.

'(When I listen to music) the one single piece of music that I get the greatest audial alcoholic high from is 'Oh Superman' by Lawrie Anderson from the 'Big Science' album.

'It has a hypnotic, trancelike effect on me. I listened to the eight minutes track ten times one night. I was compelled by it – I could not stop myself.

'In order to enlarge on (my experiences at) Melrose Avenue and Cranley Gardens I have made several attempts to strangle men. In some cases the attempts were foiled by the struggle or escape of the subject. In others I did not have the heart or desire to carry through the task. In all of the latter cases the subject was already unconscious. These persons although heavily confused the next day, were aware of painful throats and noticed their bloodshot eyes. There are at least three such men at large from the Cranley Gardens experience.

'Whatever any future court may decide, I would like you to believe the truth – that I did not maliciously plan any of the acts which form the basis of this case. In clear conscience, I could never contemplate the commissioning of any act of assault against any person or living creature. My remorse is of the deep and personal kind which will eat away inside me for the rest of my life. I am, tragically, a private person not given to public tears. The enormity of the act has left me in permanent shock.

'The trouble was that my activity increased so did the unbearable pressures which could only be escaped from by taking the best routes to oblivion via the bottle. I have slain my own dragon as surely as the press and public will slay me. They all need to see the forces of law and order slay a dragon or monster occasionally, even if the dragon is only a myth.'

That letter, written to the police officers, began by saying, 'Dear Sirs, I thank you sincerely for all your professional efforts in trying to unravel the multiplicity of detailed evidence and facts pertinent to solving the mysteries of enigmas surrounding this unfortunate, serious and monumental case.'

It ended with a quotation from *The Ballad of Reading Gaol* (Part I, iii) by Oscar Wilde:

> Yet each man kills the things he loves,
> By each let this be heard,
> Some do it with a bitter look,
> Some with a flattering word.
> The coward does it with a kiss,
> The brave man with a sword.

And he signed the missive, 'Sadly, Dennis Nilsen, H.M. Prison, Brixton.'

What could be made of all that? He was obviously well read, fluent, but now he wanted to persuade the judge and jury that he did not murder anyone – that is to kill with malice aforethought – but only killed them by reason of diminished responsibility. He claims that. Was it possible that by day Nilsen was a respectable and respected civil servant, carrying out his duties with increased reliability, but by night, and only on some nights, could kill but only with diminished responsibility?

Nilsen's memory varied, but he led the police through a catalogue of murder in some detail, and even when he could not remember a precise date, or a name, he could at least give some salient facts. Nilsen recalled that he killed first at the Christmas of 1978, a year before the first murder recorded on the charge sheet of the court. The reason for the omission was that the police have never been able to identify the victim.

He had lived in Melrose Avenue since November, 1975, and several young men had lived with him there. One by one they left and by the Christmas of 1978 he was feeling very lonely and very miserable. He spent Christmas on his own, alone with his dog, and on December 29 went to look for company. He went to the Cricklewood Arms and drank pint after pint of draught Guinness which was not normally his drink.

Even in a Christmas pub he was very much alone. Everyone was in a convivial group and only at the end of the night did he get into conversation with a young Irishman who was also on his own. They went back to Melrose Avenue where 'we had a damn good drink. Later on I remember thinking he would probably be going soon – another ship passing in the night. In the morning he was lying on top of the bed fully clothed. I was on the other bed. He was dead and I came to the conclusion that I had killed him.'

Nilsen thus began rationalizing his actions in chronological order. He had a 'sort of desperation for company. I wanted company over the New Year.' The Irishman wanted to go and Nilsen wanted him to stay. 'My tie was round his neck,' said Nilsen simply, but he then went into the grey area of recollection. 'I think I started off with about fifteen ties. I have only got one left, a clip-on.'

There had been no argument, no recollection of any struggle. It could have been any time – one o'clock, two o'clock, three o'clock, four o'clock, he did not know. 'In the morning for a long period of time I just stood there shocked. I was horrified, it was the first time anything like this had happened.'

Although Nilsen had had training in butchery dur-ing his service with the Army Catering Corps he did not mutilate his first victim. He put the body in two plastic bags and concealed it under the floorboards, surrounded by bricks and dirt, and there he kept it from the early hours of December 30, 1978, for eight months until August of 1979, when he burned it, still fully clothed, at the bottom of the garden. He burned some rubbish at the same time to mask the smell. 'It was a relief at the end of a very sorry period,' he said.

The Nilsen pattern of murder, if it deserved such a title, was thrown out of contour in the case of the second victim. No drifter, no alcoholic, no degenerate begging in the gutter, but a healthy, personable young tourist from Canada, Kenneth Ockenden. Ockenden was staying at the Central Hotel, Argyll Street, King's Cross, and, using the Egon Ronay good pub guide, chose the Princess Louise in Holborn.

Nilsen met him there at lunch time. They chatted, went sightseeing and bought £20 worth of drink to take back to Melrose Avenue. Ockenden insisting on contributing his share of the drinks bill, and they sat down to a meal. Then they listened to music, first Nilsen, then Ockenden. Nilsen remembered giving the phones to Ockenden as they sat drinking. 'All right?' asked Nilsen.

'Bloody good this – fantastic!' he replied and became engrossed in the records.

Nilsen thought, 'Bloody good guest, this. I thought he would be there all night. I turned the television up loud.' But Ockenden just sat there listening through the earphones. Nilsen said, 'Let me listen to the music as well . . .'

Nilsen remembered then sometime after midnight dragging Ockenden across the floor with the flex of the earphones still round his neck. 'I put the dog out because he was barking. Ockenden was lying on the floor. I untangled the phones, put the earphones on and listened to the whole sequence of records. In the morning the record player was still going round but I had been asleep. I don't actually remember putting the cord round his neck. I just climbed into the bunk and crashed out.'

Nilsen slept until the next evening. He had to reassure his pet, Bleep, that everything was all right, for unlike the master the dog was very frightened. He put the Canadian's body under the floorboards fully clothed, covered it with bricks and earth and left it there. By and by he found the music irksome and so he smashed three records that the visitor had been listening to, shovelled them on to a spade and threw them outside. 'It reminded me of the incident,' he said.

If there ever was a clear-cut motive Nilsen was not aware of it. It certainly was not gain. Ockenden wore a money belt in which there were Canadian dollars. The killer tore them up, but he did not destroy all tell-tale possessions, an omission which helped police solve murder Number Three, that of Martyn Duffey, who was only sixteen at the time of his death and possibly the youngest victim.

Duffey from Birkenhead had begun a course of catering at the local technical college and had a set of knives and other implements with his name engraved on them. They were with him when he left home on May 13, 1980, to go to live in New Brighton in the Wirral. Yet four days later Duffey turned up in London. Nilsen had been at a Civil and Public Services Association trade union conference at Southport, Lancashire, while Duffey had moved from his original home to New Brighton, Cheshire, on the mouth of the Mersey. New Brighton and Southport, on either side of that river, are only fifteen miles apart.

It seems too much of a coincidence that they should have met within one day of Nilsen being in the north-west. He cannot remember anything about the meeting, whether it was on the Mersey, on the train travelling south or by chance in London, but he did remember a lot about Duffey, that he had been in trouble with the police, that he had had psychiatric treatment, and appeared, to Nilsen, to have a persecution complex.

The trade union conference ended on Friday, May 16, 1980, and within twenty-four hours Duffey had travelled with him either by taxi or underground train to Willesden and Melrose Avenue. 'We probably met in a pub when I was out drinking heavily,' said Nilsen.

In those days the layout of Nilsen's flat was different to what it became. It was one huge room and he had built a large platform about six feet high with a ladder up to his bed on the top. He went to bed that night and next morning got down from his bed and found Duffey dead on the floor. 'I remember next morning he was dead on the floor. I can remember bits and pieces. I don't remember any violence at all. He had my tie round his neck.'

Nilsen searched Duffey's clothing and found a left-luggage ticket issued from Euston station on Friday, May 16. He had put Duffey's body, fully clothed, under the floorboards. Then when the smell became too great he took up both Duffey's and Ockenden's bodies and dissected them with Duffey's knives on the stone floor of the kitchen. He put pieces of the bodies in suitcases, and the heads in carrier bags, placing everything in the shed which he had had built in case Bleep, his pet, had puppies. Around the bodies he built a brick barrier and covered them with bricks and magazines and there they stayed throughout the summer of 1980. The shed door was not locked. No one complained, because Nilsen said, 'I monitored the situation', spraying the bodies once a day with disinfectant.

Towards the end of that year he took out the bodies and burned them in the garden.

The fourth victim was William Sutherland, the twenty-five-year-old male prostitute from Granton, Edinburgh. He had been married and divorced. His mother and a girl friend described him as a heavy drinker. He led a 'gipsy life', and while plying his trade as a male prostitute in the West End, he met Nilsen in a public house near to the Pleasure-U amusement arcade. When Nilsen walked to Piccadilly underground to take a train home Sutherland followed him and said, 'I have got nowhere to go.' Nilsen was not very enthusiastic at the obvious approach but paid Sutherland's fare and took him back to Melrose Avenue. There they started drinking. 'We had a great binge and I killed Billy Sutherland. I remember having a tie round his neck and pulling. I don't recall him struggling but I think he must have done.'

Nilsen, even as he told the story, took a step backwards and said, 'As casually as that. I did it from the front.'

Considering the relative sizes of his victims Nilsen escaped unharmed from most encounters. Asked if he had ever been punched, bruised or scratched he claimed that he found his strength increased two or three times when he had been drinking. His victims, however, must have been in a comatose state, unless they were securely bound, for there are very few recorded cases of murder in which a killer has strangled an unwilling victim from the front.

After killing Sutherland, Nilsen went to bed. He could not recall when he put the body under the floor but it may have been a couple of days later, indicating again that he had lived in the flat, gone about his domestic chores, with a complete corpse for company. When he felt like it he would put the body under the

162

floorboards. He could not recall how many would be there. 'I am not sure. I did not do a stock check or anything.'

But he later dissected the body and put it in a suitcase in the garden shed. It was burned in the fire which Nilsen had at the end of the year.

Early in 1981 when Billy had not been in touch with his folk in Edinburgh his mother did not formally report him as a missing person but contacted the Salvation Army. For once, however, they did not succeed in tracing their quarry – because he was dead, dissected, in a suitcase or on the funeral pyre.

The fifth victim, like the first, has never been identified. Therefore Nilsen was not charged with his murder. But Nilsen remembers him as being in his twenties, with a half-European, half-Mexican or half-Philippino appearance. Nilsen met him as he left the Salisbury public house in St Martin's Lane, Trafalgar Square, in the autumn of 1980. 'I did not buy him drinks. I was accosted by him. I left the Salisbury and he followed. He came back to Melrose Avenue. I remember the next day he was dead and I probably strangled him, but the details I cannot remember. It is academic.'

He put the body under the floor and 'I must have dissected it later.'

The sixth victim, like the first and the fifth, was also unknown. Another Irishman, in his late twenties, but living locally in the Willesden area. Nilsen met him in the Cricklewood Arms and the victim became just another number.

'Next morning there was another body in the flat. My impression was that I had strangled him because he had marks on his neck. I put him under the floorboards straight away before *rigor mortis* set in. I dismembered the body in the kitchen, and put the remains in the garden shed.'

The first, fifth, sixth and now the seventh were all unidentified, and the seventh was perhaps the most pathetic of all the victims. He was an emaciated young man, according to Nilsen, his facial features pale, hollow and withdrawn. He was 'grossly undernourished' with a long ragged trench-coat, ridiculously over-long baggy trousers, probably obtained from some social relief centre. All he had was a carrier bag. He looked like a vagrant. Nilsen spoke to him as he tried to hail a taxi home to Melrose Avenue and asked him why he was hanging about in Oxford Street.

The pathetic stranger said he was living rough so Nilsen invited him home. They caught the taxi together. 'He said he was starving,' said Nilsen. 'I plied him some food and some coffee. He was not interested in alcohol. He said he was tired and dozed off in a chair.'

Nilsen, that night, was heading for a musical and alcoholic high. As the man slept the host began drinking Bacardi, listened to Rick Wakeman's 'Criminal Record' and Laurie Anderson's 'Oh Superman'. That was when Nilsen remembered that 'because of the effects of music and alcohol, I felt exhilarated. I was on some type of high.'

The suddenly invigorated Nilsen went to the cupboard, took a tie and began to strangle the man.

'I put the tie round twice – double round his neck. I slowly pulled it tight with both hands. I do not remember any sound. There was no movement at first. But then his legs lifted and separated. They kept doing this in the air, as if he was riding a bike.'

Nilsen reckoned it took about ninety seconds to kill him. 'I had no feeling of urgency about it. I carried on for another thirty seconds, then let go. I did not believe

I had killed him so quickly. It was like taking candy from a baby. I remember thinking, "You will have no more troubles now, squire." I felt I was doing him a favour. I felt his life was one long struggle. I believed I was in a quasi-god role. I thought I could do anything I wanted.'

He put the body under the floorboards, but it was so small. 'It went on to the fire wrapped up like a package in brown paper. I could not cut him up. He was too frail. I could not look at him. It reminded me of concentration camps.'

Nilsen had reached the half-way mark in his catalogue of murder, and he waxed philosophical about it all. 'Many people have come to Melrose Avenue but only a tiny percentage came to any grief. I could put someone under the floorboards and I could forget them and meet new people afterwards.'

But another mystery remained: who was and who was not to be a victim?

'People who need me are going to be victims,' he claimed at one stage, but that meant people who desperately needed company, food or drink. Ockenden, the Canadian, did not need him, so when asked the question again he said, 'We are getting into the realms of psychiatry. I don't know.'

He built large bonfires on waste ground at the rear of 195 Melrose Avenue, burned the contents of the suitcases and carrier bags containing the victims' heads on it. Then he put a tyre from a car on it to mask any smells of burning flesh. Afterwards he would rake over the remains so that nothing would show.

There seemed, from his own words, to be an air of finality about the big bonfire at the end of 1980 but the killings were by no means finished. Victim No. 8 was also unidentified and again no charge could be made. Nilsen said he had met the young man, aged between twenty-five and thirty, late in 1980, after the big bonfire. He wore long hippie-style hair, denim jacket and jeans. It was after a night's drinking. 'Much drink flowed,' said Nilsen.

Then, remembering him, almost nonchalantly he said, 'I first became conscious about his presence when I saw he was dead with a rope round his neck.' There followed the now familiar ritual. Nilsen dismembered the body, packaged it, put it under the floorboards and later removed it to be burned.

So far much of the inventory had concerned the unknown, anonymous, victims in a vacuum, whom no one had missed, about whom no one cared. But the next intended victim survived and became the first key witness to indicate that the mass killer was telling the truth, or as near to the truth as a human being could expect. Because he survived, he complained to the police and the police had not pursued his complaint (he said). Now Nilsen was telling the police everything, the witness would have to be believed. So he was called to the Old Bailey to tell the judge and jury just what happened when Nilsen invited him home on November 10, 1980.

Douglas Stewart, the chef from Thurso in the north of Scotland, from Northwood, Middlesex, and more recently from the Holland Park Hotel, Notting Hill, just had to be believed.

Twelve

The ninth victim, Nilsen thought he killed in early 1981. He was Scottish, aged between eighteen and twenty, and Nilsen met him in the Golden Lion in Dean Street. They had returned by taxi to Melrose Avenue, engaged in a heavy drinking session until after midnight when 'I remember sitting on top of him and strangling him.'

At the moment of truth the young man had urinated and Nilsen's own trousers had become wet at the same time.

With supreme indifference Nilsen went to work next morning leaving the body under a kitchen blanket.

About a month later Nilsen met his tenth victim, a man in his mid-twenties, and presumably after the usual West End encounter had returned to Melrose Avenue. 'I found the body on the floor in the sitting room. I don't remember anything round his neck.' The body had been put under the floorboards with the two others and the civil servant summed it up. 'That was it. Floorboards back. Carpets replaced. And back to work at Denmark Street.'

The eleventh victim was also unidentified and met his fate after yet another month's lapse. A skinhead with a London accent, aged between seventeen and twenty-one, he met him after closing time in Leicester Square. The two had taken a taxi to the Nilsen home.

'We had many drinks. I got the impression he looked a good drinker. He boasted about how tough he was and how much he could drink. I told him I was an under-exercised clerical pen-pusher. After drinking, the man flaked out. I didn't think he was very tough. I removed my tie and put it round his neck and strangled him.

'End of the day. End of drinking. End of a person.'

While the killer could try to reason about his motives he was beginning to have difficulty with the practicalities of disposal. He tied the eleventh victim with string, put it under the flooring, but had difficulty wedging it in. What worried Nilsen, though, was not only the smell but the fear of discovery. Three bodies under the floorboards at this stage had not been dismembered and they were becoming what he described as 'a slight smell problem to a critical one'. In addition, in June, 1981, someone broke into Nilsen's flat and vandalized the contents. What if the burglar had found the bodies?

Nilsen solved the problem by taking up the bodies, removing their clothes, dissecting them and putting them back.

His stay at Melrose Avenue was drawing to a close. He found his twelfth victim, Malcolm Barlow, the twenty-three-year-old vagrant, of low intelligence and epileptic, from Rotherham sitting on the pavement in Melrose Avenue. He said he had had a fit and could not move his legs. Nilsen invited him inside. Later, on September 17, 1981, Barlow was admitted for treatment at the Middlesex Hospital. Afterwards Nilsen found him on his doorstep, invited him in to share a meal, watch television and have a drink. Barlow had three drinks.

'Much later on I was engrossed in watching television. I went to the divan to rouse Barlow but he was unconscious. I thought he might die on the spot. I was slapping his face to wake him up but there was no response. After about twenty minutes I decided what to do. I put my hands round his throat and held my position for two to three minutes. Not feeling much like prising up the floorboards, I dragged him into the kitchen and put him under the sink.

'Killing him seemed right at the time. In some cases I am aware that at the precise moment of the act I believe I am right in doing the act. If there was a bomb blast at the time nothing would have stopped me.'

Then the night before he left Melrose Avenue for Cranley Gardens there was the third bonfire. 'On to the fire went the remains of four victims under the floorboards plus Malcolm Barlow's body, which had been under the kitchen sink.' To help the task Nilsen had taken a garden roller to crush the bones still further before consigning them to the flames.

'Driving away from 195 Melrose Avenue was a great relief. Being on a top floor at Cranley Gardens I thought it would change things. Yes I did. I thought up here you won't get into any mischief. Unfortunately that was not the case.'

Victims Numbers 13, 14 and 15 were all killed there, but first there was another who got away, Paul Nobbs, the language student from Bushey, Watford, Hertford-shire and Lancaster University. A homosexual, he used the Golden Lion public house in Dean Street, met Nilsen there one lunch time and returned with him to Cranley Gardens for a meal. They watched television and Nobbs telephoned his mother at home in Bushey to say he was staying the night with a friend. They went into the bedroom and undressed. They mastur-bated each other. Nobbs then tried to penetrate Nilsen from behind, but Nilsen said, 'No, don't,' and muttered something about being a virgin.

When Nobbs got up at 6 a.m. he noticed the marks on his throat and went to see the doctor. He told his doctor and his mother that he had been strangled in

169

the street by muggers. He thought no one would believe his story so he did not tell the police. He still went to the Golden Lion. He still saw Nilsen but he did not speak to him.

As for Nilsen, he remembered Nobbs, recalled having had a lot to drink and putting a tie round Nobbs' neck, but 'I was panicky. I remembered trying to revive him because his heart was still beating and I threw a glass of water over him.' Then with superb irony Nilsen told him he should see a doctor and stop drinking.

The incident provided an insight into the sexual side of Nilsen. He could remember Nobbs, remember drinking, remember putting a tie round his neck, but sex? 'I can't remember. It's quite possible. I don't like pleasures I can't remember.' If, as Nobbs suggested, he refused anal sex, was he in fact a homosexual? 'In the accepted terms,' said Nilsen, 'no. Because I have had relationships with male and female. My predominant attraction was male. I don't deny I have had relations of a homosexual nature. But with every single victim in this case, I never engaged in sexual intercourse with them before or after death.'

Not surprisingly Nilsen found that not all his victims succumbed so easily. John the Guardsman – John Peter Howlett – was not only difficult to kill but was eventually subdued in one of the most chilling accounts provided by the killer. He had met Howlett twice in December, 1981, and again in March, 1982, in the Golden Lion. Howlett was taken back to Cranley Gardens where he drank large quantities of Bacardi and Coca Cola.

When Howlett was in bed, Nilsen said, 'I got hold of a loose upholstery strap. I wound the material round his neck. He fought back furiously. He was a very fit person. Summoning all my strength I forced him back down. He hit his head on the bedrail and seemed to go limp but he was still breathing. I tightened my grip for another minute or so round his neck. I was shaking all over but found he was still breathing. I was shocked.

'I held on for another two or three minutes. His heart was still beating. I couldn't believe it. I pulled him to the bathroom and pushed him over the rim. I put the plug in and ran the water. I held him for four or five minutes. I went to bed shaking.

'I left the body in the bath until next morning and then left it in the bedroom for a day or two. I had to dispose of it because a friend was due to come on a visit.'

Nilsen dissected the body, flushed pieces down the lavatory but 'this proved a slow process so I decided to boil some of it, including the head. I put all the large bones out with the rubbish and other pieces into the tea chest.'

The fourteenth was Graham Allan, aged twenty-eight, from Newarthill, Glasgow, identified, but not the subject of a murder charge. Nilsen met Allan, who had had a row with his girl friend, took him home from Shaftesbury Avenue. Nilsen made him an omelette, then Allan 'slumped forward unconscious from fatigue and drink. I remember going forward and he was dead. I don't know whether the omelette killed him but in going forward I intended to kill him and an omelette doesn't leave red marks on the neck.'

Stephen Sinclair, the epileptic from Perth, Scotland, was the fifteenth and last victim. Sinclair was also on drugs. They saw the sign, 'There's a welcome at Macdonalds', in Oxford Street and went in for hamburgers. They had been drinking heavily and bought more whisky and lager to take to Cranley Gardens. Nilsen listened to the rock opera, 'Tommy', on his stereo earphones. Sinclair went to sleep. 'I cannot remember anything else until I woke up next day. He was in the armchair, dead. On the floor was a piece of string with a tie attached to it.'

Again he was asked: Why? 'I don't know. I have been trying to work it out. I am not a head shrinker. Everyone keeps walking out on me. I drink to relieve the pressure. I think I am a chronic alcoholic. Even after drinking a bottle of Bacardi I can still talk rationally. I may not remember afterwards but I am okay.

'I took Steve Sinclair from the cupboard where I had originally put him, laid him on a plastic sheet on the carpet and cut off his head with a long kitchen knife. I put the head into the pot, put the lid on it and lit the stove. When the head was coming to the boil I turned the pot down to simmer. Then I took the dog for a walk.'

Nilsen was almost finished. 'If I had not been arrested until I was sixty-five there might have been a thousand bodies. I could never have a permanent relationship with anyone, but I felt it was a situation I could handle.' He thought like that after each murder. He could not remember what had prompted him to kill the last victim, yet 'I knew it would happen again. I was resigned to the fact that it would happen again. And I would get caught eventually but I would do the best I could to dispose of the evidence.'

It was, in fact, the disposal, by way of the lavatory and the drains, that proved his undoing. Even then, with considerable gall, he wrote to the managing agents of the property in Cranley Gardens complaining that the lavatories would not flush because of some blockage in the drains. The man from Dyno-rod came, as did the police and the truth was out. Or was it? The truth about Nilsen seemed to be that he was a mass killer but there remained the question: Why?

Nilsen's plea that he was not guilty of murder but

172

only guilty of manslaughter because of diminished responsibility is worth looking at in the light of some of his attitudes as well as his words. On the morning after he tried to kill the student Paul Nobbs 'he seemed no different at all,' said Nobbs. 'In fact he was perhaps more jocular than before.' Nobbs, a confessed homosexual, added that 'at first I thought perhaps Nilsen is gay, perhaps he is not. I couldn't be sure.' He had not engaged in any sadistic, masochistic or bondage activity, nor had he tried to force any drinks on his intended victims.

Carl Le Fox, who went to the Old Bailey using his real name of Carl Stotter, retold how Nilsen tried to kill him. 'He still seemed a very nice person, very caring, interested in what I was talking about.' When Carl told him about his fight with his friend in Blackpool he added, 'I wish I was dead.' To which Nilsen replied, 'Don't be silly. You have your whole life in front of you.' And then Nilsen tried to strangle him with the zip of the sleeping bag and when that failed tried to drown him, but he gave no sign of being aware of having done anything to harm Carl.

'I think it was odd that after nearly killing me, Desi was as calm and friendly as he had been before the incident.' Prior to the attack he had done nothing at all to upset Desi who had not said 'Sorry' or shown any sign of remorse.

At the same time, no one came forward to confirm the tales of people like Hunter-Craig or Lamont; although Nilsen himself confirmed a minor point of Hunter-Craig's story. 'I turned away a man from the flat from Exeter I had met once previously' – not regularly for eleven months but once previously – 'I could obviously not admit him when Stephen Sinclair's headless naked body was lying on the floor in my front room.'

When the police came he surprised Detective Chief Inspector Jay by his manner. He had never come across a case in which someone was so willing immediately to cooperate. Nilsen offered samples of blood, hair and clothing if it would help. He even offered to go over police photographs of missing people to see if he could identify any of them as his victims.

If Nilsen had had pressures which forced him to kill, what were they? He certainly faced greater responsibility at work after being promoted from a clerical officer to an executive officer. He was also branch secretary of the Civil and Public Services Association trade union. One union official told the police that Nilsen wanted to do a good job for his members and had a social conscience. He did not like people being exploited, and was a man of principle. Nilsen ran the branch well, looked after his members and was one of the civil service trade union's better branch secretaries.

He was very union orientated and during the time he was branch secretary he had been under pressure because the work was on top of his Job Centre duties.

Jay, the experienced policeman, was sickened by the tale Nilsen told him about fifteen or sixteen murders, and the horrifying way in which the bodies were disposed of, but Nilsen was passive and calm, extremely self possessed. The only feeling about another living creature he showed was about his dog, Bleep. His dog was very important to him. It had been his permanent companion for a long time.

As a result Jay found it very difficult to match the man who was talking about murder and the man who was devoted to his dog. The prisoner who one moment would tell Jay about his pet black and white mongrel was the next saying, in the same tone of voice, 'I killed them by strangulation. I get nothing from inflicting pain. It is just compulsion when I am drunk. It was quick. I cut up the bodies on plastic sheeting in the front room. I am a trained butcher. I have got qualifications that make me familiar with the digestive system and the circulatory system. I would have known what I was doing.'

Then his memory would fail again. 'When you go on the piss you can't remember. When I drank a Bacardi at home I would go out... Pass out. As for disposing of them, you could dissect them, boil the bits, and the flesh would come away from the bones. You can dispose of the bones in the normal rubbish without being suspected.' He kept a pot in which to boil the pieces, in which he had also boiled the three skulls, the pot he bought for the curry he made for the Christmas party for his colleagues at the Job Centre.

Remorse? Reason? 'I don't know. I have been trying to work it out. I am not a head shrinker. Everyone keeps walking out on me. I drink to relieve the pressure. I think I am a chronic alcoholic.'

How many times did he kill? How many times did he try to kill? He had tried unsuccessfully to kill seven people. 'People have woken up in my flat with marks round their necks and asked me what had happened. Police were called a couple of times and allegations made, but nothing happened.' He succeeded, even without all the identifications, in killing fifteen people. The circumstantial evidence of his recollections or actual identification are not disputed. The mystery devolves on his declaration made in the police car on the way to the station after his arrest when asked how many bodies. He replied, 'Sixteen.' So accurate, so exact on so many matters, it has always seemed illogical that he should have given that figure. Instantly. Without hesitation.

All men boast and mass murderers are no exception. The annals of criminology are studded with discrepancies between the number of people murderers claim to have murdered and the number of crimes they are actually proved to have committed. But there is something bedevilling about the figure sixteen, although the jury were not to hear it.

The figure, if true, would have made Dennis Andrew Nilsen the greatest mass murderer in British history. That unrespected list has for more than one hundred years belonged to Mary Ann Cotton, the thrice-married former nurse of County Durham. In 1871 she went with her bigamous husband, Frederick, his two stepsons and her own six-month-old baby. Within two months Frederick died at the age of sixty-nine with gastric fever. Not long afterwards one of Mary's lovers, Joseph Natrass, moved in as a lodger. Meanwhile Mary had become pregnant again, this time by a local excise officer, Quick-Manning.

Within the twenty-two days between March 10 and April 1, 1872, three more deaths occurred in the house. Natrass, her own young baby of some months, and her late husband's eldest child, a boy of ten. On July 12 the other stepson of Frederick died and a suspicious neighbour called on the local constable. The doctor refused to issue a death certificate. A post-mortem examination showed, after analysis of the stomach contents, the presence of arsenic.

Cotton was charged with murder of the stepson, taken to Durham Prison, where her child by Quick-Manning was born. At her trial in March, 1873, she pleaded Not Guilty, claimed that the dead boy had been poisoned accidentally by arsenic contained in green floral wallpaper used in the home. She could not, however, account for her purchase of soft soap and arsenic, except to say it was for cleaning bedsteads and destroying bedbugs. She was found Guilty and sentenced to death.

The fact that her baby was taken from her five days before her execution was responsible for a gathering expression of sentimentality, a demand for her reprieve from the gallows. The Home Secretary refused. The hangman botched the hanging for she jerked for three whole minutes on the end of the rope before the so-called instantaneous death took place. The date was March 24, 1873.

Twenty-one persons had died while in close association with Mary, but the police and criminologists have limited her total of suspected murders to fourteen or fifteen. Her motive was understandable. Each time there was a death she stood to collect insurance money and that was very useful as she planned her next, new marriage.

To exceed her achievement, within the bounds of possibility, Nilsen had to make it sixteen.

Thirteen

The answer to all the riddles of Dennis Andrew Nilsen are in his mind. Those who tried to probe his psyche found some of the answers. Nilsen, according to his own fancy, had tried to help them. He had, with unbelievable difficulty, secured legal aid to pay the fees of not one but two psychiatrists. One is Dr James Alexander Culpin MacKeith of the Interim Secure Unit at Bethlem Royal Hospital which is closely linked with the Maudsley in psychiatric work among prisoners. Dr MacKeith is also consultant to Broadmoor Hospital, Crowthorne, Berkshire, which houses criminal psychiatric patients. The other psychiatrist is Dr Patrick Lionel Grattan Gallwey, consultant forensic psychiatrist to the South West Thames regional hospital authority, and to prisons like Wandsworth and, formerly, Wormwood Scrubs.

Nilsen, in his anxiety to help, wrote to Dr MacKeith a letter under the heading, 'Mental Condition'. In it he said, 'I have felt since my teenage days that I am a creative psychopath. When I am under pressure or drunk, dormant feelings are released. I can't look back, only forward. I deserve to be punished. In a strange way I think (the risky dismembering and disposal of bodies) became part of the wish to be caught. I was at a tense breaking point, waiting to be caught so that I could be released from guilt.'

At another point Nilsen wrote, 'I have an overwhelming desire to kill. But the strong side of my moral character should have produced the power to

178

resist. I cannot allow the buck to travel outside my responsibility. I deserve punishment for their deaths.'

Even at such a late stage of self-examination Nilsen found it necessary to go into the details of individual cases, like that of his last victim, Stephen Sinclair, the epileptic, the sick young man from Perth. 'I would have liked to have a long social and sexual relationship with him.' Nilsen recalled that he had washed Sinclair's body, laid it out, and imagined himself lying next to it on a mortuary slab. He believed that Stephen and the other victims would have forgiven him. Even though he masturbated over their corpses.

Dr McKeith believed that Nilsen may have been more concerned about his power of life and death than a simple intention to kill. His belief that he was godlike reflected a phenomenon in the Biblical quotation, 'the Lord giveth and the Lord taketh away'. As Nilsen had said, 'Dead bodies fascinated me, but I would have done anything to have them back alive. The greater the beauty of the man the greater the sense of loss and grief.'

The psychiatrist had asked Nilsen about his life-long loneliness, his drinking bouts and blackouts, his obsession with nakedness and unconsciousness, which led him to masturbate over the corpses in a symbolic gesture of farewell. He came to the conclusion that the mass killer was paranoid and unsure of his own identity and desperate for the attention of others. Nilsen adopted a grandiose air which was apparent in the way he picked up people, escorted them to his home and entertained them before killing them.

Nilsen told Dr MacKeith that they would sit down and Nilsen would take up the position of an auctioneer in a verbal saleroom of subjects which he would put up, like art, music, politics, Mrs Thatcher, all completely cynical. If they entered into the spirit of the rather one-sided debate, then it was all right by Nilsen. If they did not, and fell asleep, they would be dead already. Nilsen thought 'that his audience didn't care about anything. They just struggled along from day to day. I was giving them a chance to live.'

Nilsen's personality disorder, in Dr MacKeith's view, stemmed from the first feelings of loneliness, from the time his father, an unreliable parent who drank heavily, left the family home when Nilsen was only three years of age. Nilsen had grown close to his mother's father, Andrew Whyte, but that grandfather died three years later, when Nilsen had just reached his seventh birthday. 'He sought his grandfather out and went looking for him, although at another level, he knew his grandfather was dead,' the doctor reported.

The boy resented his mother's remarriage when he was ten years old and he became extremely withdrawn. Then began the catalogue of friendships which were broken. Although he gave other reasons to other people, Nilsen told the doctor that his decision to leave the army after ten or eleven years was because a young fellow soldier did not return his affections.

How much Dr MacKeith believed is less important than that people understand the two sides to Nilsen, the fact and the fantasy. In Nilsen's sexual development he had built up a 'library' of bizarre stories, some of which were true, but some of which were untrue although Nilsen believed them. One was that when he was in adolescence a boy of sixteen had stripped him naked. So did a taxi driver, but he later killed the taxi driver. No trace of such a murder has been found.

As a young man Nilsen covered his body with talcum powder so that he looked like a corpse and masturbated in front of mirrors. He had also covered his victims with powder and looked at their naked whiteness in a mirror. Or so Nilsen said.

After leaving the army Nilsen had embarked on a phase of extreme promiscuous homosexuality (although Nilsen's own accounts of the extent of his homosexuality – companionship, fondling, kissing, cuddling, masturbation without penetration – have varied considerably). Nilsen, in a rare confession to Dr MacKeith, talked about the sexual fantasies which troubled his mind, particularly fantasies of sexually assaulting children and a female relative. He was similarly frightened by black-outs following heavy drinking sessions. On one occasion, in 1976, he claimed that he had 'lost himself' for five hours and found himself in a strange part of London.

There were two Nilsens, the truthful man and the fantasy-maker, just as there were two Nilsens, one at home and one at work. He was able to maintain an appearance of normality at work while at home, since 1978, he had been dealing with the dreadful problem of the bodies, their smell and their disposal. If anyone wanted evidence of this they had only to ask the survivors like Stewart, Nobbs and Stotter who all remembered his calm, pleasant manner despite his violence and threats of violence.

Nilsen's fluency did not surprise the psychiatrist, but he noted that Nilsen thought of himself as famous without appreciating that he was in fact notorious. In talking about himself to the doctor he became grandiose, treating the doctor almost as if he was one of the victims – in the sense that Nilsen does not believe anyone listens to him. Even his relatives, he complained, did not listen to him. He had asked them for photographs of his young nephews and nieces. (A possible explanation for their refusal is that Nilsen has also asked his family for personal histories, nicknames and the like for the purpose of his biography, but his mother, Mrs Elizabeth Scott, has declined.)

Dr MacKeith concluded that Nilsen's impaired sense of identity meant that he was often like a film director directing himself, as a lead actor of course, from a distance. All these matters, noted by the doctor, led him to believe that Nilsen's lack of remorse coupled with the conviction that he was not mad, added up to a severe personality disorder. That meant that he was mentally ill during the four years of killing: loneliness, perverted sex-life, paranoid tendencies and craving for attention.

How else could anyone explain his stories? When he was ten years old and living by the coast in Scotland he remembers walking into the sea fully clothed, losing his footing and drowning. He recovered consciousness lying in the nearby sand dunes and he was then naked with his wet clothes beside him, neatly folded. He noticed a substance on his abdomen, thought it was semen and thought then and now that he must have been rescued by an unknown boy of sixteen whom he had seen nearby. He said he assumed that the boy masturbated over him.

When he was in the army in the Middle East he was returning to his base drunk and in a taxi. He awoke to find he was being coshed by the driver. He was bundled into the boot of the vehicle where he recovered consciousness, found he was naked and his clothes were beside him. He feared his throat would be cut. When he opened the boot he hit the man on the head with a jack and killed him and then returned to his army depot without ever reporting the incident.

Dr MacKeith came to the conclusion about a personality disorder from the sum of all the clues. No one single aspect made it possible to reach that diagnosis. 'I am not saying he is mad. I say he suffers from a severe personality disorder. All of the features amount to clear evidence of severe personality disorder. I

would describe it as of being of an unspecified type.'
For the disorder included the delusions of paranoia,
the split personality of the schizoid, the temper of the
hysterical, and the anti-social behaviour of the socio-
path.

Of course, Nilsen was consistently inconsistent.

When Dr MacKeith came to give his evidence to the
Old Bailey jury, he declared: 'I believe that if attacks
occurred they were done by another person. Half his
mind dealt with one part of the matter and a half with
another.'

Mr Green, for the prosecution, commented, 'I am not
talking about half his mind. He is a jolly good actor.'

And, as in all such cases, that was where the legal
world and the world of medicine parted.

The definition of diminished responsibility is a legal
definition. MacKeith would not say, on his oath as a
psychiatrist, that Nilsen was or was not suffering from
diminished responsibility.

The other psychiatrist, Dr Gallwey, however, said he
believed Nilsen did suffer from diminished responsibility when he committed the murders. The legal basis
of diminished responsibility includes but does not
totally comprise mental abnormality. And Dr Gallwey,
who examined Nilsen for over seven hours, found in
Nilsen 'a tendency towards grandiosity of which the
main feature was a need to control and dominate
situations. His personality disorder goes back towards
his childhood. He is appearing as somebody he is not.
His appearances of normality are not necessarily normal. It is a highly deceptive personality.

'He has an area of his life in which he behaves
perfectly normally. Alongside that he is having to keep
at bay these disturbances which are part and parcel of
a schizoid and paranoid personality. He is under
constant strain between the normal area and the

disturbed area. Although they are in equilibrium, it is potentially a very, very unstable one.'

Dr Gallwey described this condition as a 'false-self personality'. He had made a special study of this syndrome. Nilsen belonged to that syndrome. He was able to function completely normally so that the break-downs, outbursts or irrational violence, often with bizarre or quasi-sexual features, always apparently motiveless, made no sense in terms of his ordinary personality.

His ordinary personality was something he had to cling to desperately; some factors which held him together were the sense of belonging to a family, friends and the world of ordinary affectionate relation-ships. His emotional involvement with his family was never marvellous but it was all right. But then he cut himself off. He had not seen his family for ten years, so he tried to find a substitute relationship with homo-sexual men. He tried to find that relationship but failed. This, according to Dr Gallwey, was a very important factor, for 'it led to the deterioration in the orgnization of his personality so he finally broke down and began killing'.

Nilsen himself had blamed his entry into the world of mass murder on loneliness brought about by broken friendships and broken homosexual relationships. This is despite the fact that the psychiatrists found that his loneliness stemmed from a very early age, probably as early as the time when his father left home when he was three. But Nilsen harped on the live-in friends who stayed a substantial period of time and then left, like Barry Pett, like Stephen Martin, and particularly David Gallichan. Their departure, according to Nilsen, led him to murder, but some who wanted to stay were not killed.

Dr Gallwey had seen no evidence from what Nilsen

184

or anyone else had said to understand the motive behind each killing.

In this matter, the third psychiatrist, Dr Paul Michael Anthony Bowden, consultant forensic psychiatrist at the Maudsley Hospital, had an advantage. He had originally asked to see all the witnesses in the case, which the police refused. Ironically, although witnesses should not be subjected to interrogation by such experts pending trial, only such witnesses can speak knowledgeably about the behaviour of the accused which will eventually help the judge and jury to decide the issue.

Dr Bowden in fact saw a number of valuable people who were not witnesses. Like Cathy Hughes and Roger Farnham from the Job Centre of the Manpower Services Commission in which Nilsen worked. They had found Nilsen opinionated rather than aggressive. Like Gallichan, but more impressive was the interview Dr Bowden had with Trevor Simpson, of Derbyshire, who lived with Nilsen for eight days around Christmas in 1982.

Simpson's recollection was that 'Nilsen never had any Christmas decorations, no Christmas dinner, no cards from relatives – nothing. My impression of him at that stage was that he was a bit of a loner. He never had any friends. One night he got drunk and said he was going downstairs to "see the Professor". Nilsen came back after about two or three minutes. As far as I know there was no one living downstairs at the time. I thought he had a split personality. When he is sober he is sort of normal. When he gets drunk he imagines other people.

'After drinking heavily, Nilsen would sort of go very quiet. He used to grumble under his breath. I think he was suspicious of me a little.'

Simpson left the drunken, music-loving Nilsen in

'his secret world of make-believe'. But was he not lucky to be alive? Dr Gallwey could not explain why Nilsen had not killed or attempted to kill Simpson. The reason seems to be that people like Nilsen conceal a lot of what they feel. He had to because he was clinging to the normality of his civil service office like a man drowning in his own nightmares. He may have killed because of the nightmares, but just as there was no evidence that Nilsen killed homosexuals because they deserted him, or were about to desert him, so from any normal human point of view there were no motives that anyone, psychiatrists or laymen, could understand.

One might be excused for coming to the conclusion that Nilsen was merely an evil killer and that the workings of his mind were of no interest. He was intelligent, cunning, quick-witted and resourceful. When people had complained to the police that Nilsen had tried to murder them Nilsen had hoodwinked the police. Was he not trying to fool the judge, jury and the world at large? Dr MacKeith thought Nilsen hoodwinked himself.

Dr Gallwey did not believe Nilsen had tried to work a confidence trick on him, but sometimes he thought Nilsen had tried to mislead him. Nilsen had first to explain his behaviour to himself and to blame it on drink was the most obvious thing to do. Dr Gallwey did not believe that this was true. After all, in psychiatry, and particularly forensic psychiatry, doctors like Gallwey have to work with habitual liars who face severe punishment. They are bound to want to say things which might lessen the punishment. Psychiatrists must take trouble to avoid being misled.

It is like building a picture, taking the pieces of a jigsaw and seeing if they fit. In psychiatric cases they never fit perfectly but sometimes they fit in a way that is clearly convincing. The picture Dr Gallwey built was that at the time of the killings Nilsen sometimes felt that the victims had no business in his flat (even though he had invited them there) and that they had invaded his world. That is a very common experience of people who have broken down. And at the moment of the killings Nilsen was quite divorced from a normal awareness that his victims were real people with human properties. To Nilsen they had become objects, and he had broken them as objects, not as people.

Nilsen had had his fantasies, like the time he was sitting in a room with a blizzard howling outside but he had had plenty to eat; like the time he could hear music playing and he was the director and the film star. When he killed, Dr Gallwey concluded, he was no longer able to have feeling for what he was doing. He was in what the doctors call a 'dissociative state', or splitting; emotionless – but not all the time; fantasizing – but not all the time.

Nilsen liked to show off. That was the view of Dr Bowden, the visiting psychiatrist, called by the prosecution. He found the killer abnormal, a mild comment on a man who slays fifteen or sixteen people. Very abnormal, said Dr Bowden, because very, very few people commit those sort of crimes in those numbers, but he does not think that Nilsen suffers from any mental disorder.

The killer had told him that he had an overwhelming desire to kill in the cases that he remembered. The killings gave him a sense of power. He was able to transfer his feelings of criminality from his homosexuality to his killings. And he thought he was doing people a favour by killing them.

Dr Bowden said abnormality of the mind was a broader concept of mental disorder.

He said the killer displayed no evidence of suffering from arrested or retarded development of mind, neither

187

was there any inherited disorder, no mental disease and no injury that could have caused mental disorder.

According to Mr Green, the Crown's prosecuting counsel, he killed for fun and then used great cunning and bluff to cover his tracks. The defence said that he could not help it. The prosecution said, 'Oh, yes, he could.' He was able to control his actions. He was free to choose – and he did choose – who to leave alone, and who to kill, and who to reprieve, and, Mr Green said, 'no man hath greater power than this'.

He had been cunning in disposing of his victims and resourceful in dealing with the police who were called by a victim who escaped. So Mr Green insisted that he is a plausible fellow, a person who is able to bluff his way out of many a situation.

The argument, mad or bad, stretched over nine days at the Old Bailey, and the jury inside and the public outside could well be excused for any difficulty they had in understanding how so many learned people, three of them psychiatrists, could disagree so fundamentally over the mind of a self-confessed killer. The defence insisted that to do such things he 'must be out of his mind'. The prosecution said he knew that what he had done was wicked, against the law, and done deliberately. He had no diagnosable medical disorder.

Yet even in Brixton Prison, the prosecution conceded, he had been regarded as a high suicide risk. He had been put in a 'strip cell' – a cell without furniture and only a mattress on the floor – for his own protection. As he waited from February to October for his trial to take place he went first on hunger strike. That was in June. In July he spent four days in his prison cell completely naked because he refused to wear a prison uniform. During this time he slept under his bed, swore at prison officers, and finally flung his overflowing chamber pot at three of them.

Dr Gallwey had suggested that he was very close to insanity but he had something very tenacious in him which prevented him going mad.

Who were the jury to believe?

The prosecution psychiatrist was able to say that as he had spent fourteen hours with Nilsen over a long period of time he was able to base his findings on much wider evidence than that available to Dr MacKeith and Dr Gallwey. Those two doctors had seen Nilsen only over a relatively restricted period at the end of his remand in Brixton.

'I think that difference goes a long way to explain the contrasting judgements that have been made,' said Dr Bowden.

But this arose because the State had originally refused a legal aid certificate for one defence psychiatrist let alone two.

Shorn of psychiatric terms the jury's only concern was to decide whether Nilsen suffered from diminished responsibility when he committed the murders, and that was a question to be answered for each of the six murders listed on the charge sheet. If he did not so suffer he was a murderer and guilty as charged. If he did so suffer he was guilty only of manslaughter.

It was Thursday, November 3, when Mr Justice Croom-Johnson put to them the question and sent them out to consider their verdict.

Mr Lawrence, the defence counsel, had reminded the jury that the court in which they sat, the No 1 Court, was world-famous, had heard many amazing crimes but probably never one as horrible as this. Horrible yes, but there must be considerable doubt as to whether Nilsen was really all that clever in his cunning.

True, he disposed of his bodies skilfully, but he does not now seem to have been all that sharp in getting rid of their possessions. He threw out the precious set of butcher's knives belonging to Duffey, the boy from Birkenhead, and they were left to rust in the garden, but he kept the carving fork and the potato peeler, both with Duffey's initials on them. When he tried to strangle and then drown Carl Stotter he kept his intended victim's jewellery, ear-rings and a necklace.

So when police went to Cranley Gardens and then to Melrose Avenue to verify his statements they found much of the evidence waiting for them.

As for being mad, he spent much of his time in Brixton writing letters and his memoirs, and in one letter to co-author Douglas Bence included his latest poem. Perhaps some insight into the state of Nilsen's mind may be gained from these lines:

THE SINNER'S EYE*

The sinner's eye, soft shoots the jet
Upon the inward man
In pillagements, to close the net
On freedom's damned offences.
So easy are the tricks of light
This welcome, easy, beckoning sight
And on a dance, this loving eye
Of morning's fevered reckoning
A bitter sweetish sorrow
Today he's on the throne of kings
A catafalque tomorrow
And, somewhere, always doomed to cry
And fixing up his act to die
In cold, white, tiled latrines.
'Heated finish
Died together!'
End of all his scenes.

*Street talk for the drug addict's needle.

To those around him in Brixton he appeared more lonely than when he was first admitted. The only living creature for which he had any feeling was his mongrel dog, Bleep. Left in the house when he was arrested, rescued by the police and taken to Battersea Dogs' Home the creature pined for his master and within a very few days died. 'Poor mutt,' said Nilsen. His last friend had gone.

He was still looking for a friend when the jury of eight men and four women filed back to their places. The foreman answered the questions. They found Nilsen Guilty of Murder on all six counts and Guilty of attempted murder on both the other counts, and the judge sentenced him to six terms of life imprisonment with a recommendation that he be not released for twenty five years.

All Futura Books are available at your bookshop or
newsagent, or can be ordered from the following
address:
Futura Books, Cash Sales Department,
P.O. Box 11, Falmouth, Cornwall.

Please send cheque or postal order (no currency), and
allow 45p for postage and packing for the first book
plus 20p for the second book and 14p for each additional
book ordered up to a maximum charge of £1.63 in U.K.

Customers in Eire and B.F.P.O. please allow 45p for
the first book, 20p for the second book plus 14p per
copy for the next 7 books, thereafter 8p per book.

Overseas customers please allow 75p for postage and
packing for the first book and 21p per copy for each
additional book.